Scenes of Compassion

D0063098

A Responder's Guide for Dealing with Emergency Scene Emotional Crisis

by

Timothy W. Dietz, B.S., EMT-P

Scenes of Compassion

A Responder's Guide for Dealing with Emergency Scene Emotional Crisis

by

Timothy W. Dietz, B.S., EMT-P

Chevron Publishing Corporation
5018 Dorsey Hall Drive, Suite 104
Ellicott City, Maryland 21042

Cover Photo Courtesy of Woodburn Fire District

2001 by Chevron Publishing Coporation
Ellicott City, MD 21042

ISBN: 1-883581-20-6

Printed in the United States of America

We tend not to choose the unknown, which might be a shock or a disappointment or simply a little difficult to cope with. And yet it is the unknown with all its disappointments and surprises that is the most enriching.

Anne Morrow Lindbergh

Dedication

To Lisa & Josh, my two best friends.

And to Justin, who gave the ultimate sacrifice so that I may learn and share.

Scenes of Compassion

Table of Contents

Acknowledgments

I would like to acknowledge and thank those, who with their knowledge and inspiration, kindled the spirit that entered into this book.

The faculty of Warner Pacific College, in Portland, Oregon, whose energy, enthusiasm, compassion and dedication gave me the tools and motivation to put my experiences on paper.

Dr. Jeffrey T. Mitchell and Dr. George S. Everly, whose dedicated research and work keeps those of us in the emergency services field mentally healthy and able to continue in occupations we love. They, along with the International Critical Incident Stress Foundation staff, are to be commended for their efforts.

Emergency responders, regardless of discipline, who give the extra effort to see that survivors of tragedy are taken care.

Prologue:

An Autobiography of Scene Compassion

I love the emergency services: the camaraderie, the excitement, the chance to really be wanted and needed by people you don't know and the opportunity to use physical and mental abilities against the forces of evil and death. Along with this "heroic" image however comes the fact that people die. From chronic disease to random acts of violence, from the newborn infant to the elderly, in this career you will see that death does not discriminate. That is the focus of this book, because during the first six years of my career that is what I did; I saw death. Even though I tried to avoid it, I saw the grieving parent clutch the dead child, and I saw the elderly woman beg her deceased husband of 60 years to take just one more breath. And there I stood, along with the other firefighters and medics, hoping that a relative or anybody, would show up and sit with these "survivors" so that we could get back to the safety of the fire station. Fortunately those of us in the emergency services know that the satisfaction and good of the job far overpowers and outweighs the occasional tragedy. But it does not make the tragedies easier when they are occurring.

I had just been promoted and was moving into a new house when I became a "survivor." My youngest son drowned in a bathtub at the baby-sitters. Since I was unpacking at the new house, my wife, who was packing at the old house, was the first to be notified and went to the scene. Several weeks after this incident, my wife and I were driving and she saw one of the emergency workers who responded to my son's incident, driving in another car. She became visibly angry and upset. It was then that she shared with me her experience at the scene and the emergency workers' actions in dealing (by restraint) with her. It became apparent to me the deep and profound impact that we as emergency responders have on surviving family members. When I returned to work, I began to consciously take a look at how surviving family members were being treated at death or dying scenes; and believe me it was not pretty. We stumble through words and actions beyond belief. We attempt to avoid, give false information, or even restrain parents who have lost a child, a wife who had lost a husband, or a child who has just seen a parent seriously injured or who has died. These "survivors" not only lose a loved one, but gain a permanent impression of brutality, non-compassion, ineptitude, and lack of understanding and support by us, the heroic emergency responders.

I realize that it is not typically an emergency responders responsibility to do a death notification. But what I do realize is that occasionally we are the only people on the scene when that family member shows up and wants to know what is happening. I also found out that this initial encounter lasts a lifetime. Why aren't emergency workers trained to understand this vital role we play at scenes of death? The excuses are numerous. In communicating with training institutions, the reasons vary from "we don't have room in the degree program," to "we don't want emergency responders to become too wrapped up in someone else's emotions." Because of this, few colleges address the significance of dealing with significant others. It is usually not until emergency workers find themselves in a position of having to deal with a grieving relative, that they decide this type of education is necessary. As a peer counselor for stress debriefings, I see the frustration and pain that grieving relatives have on unprepared responders.

This book will offer the education and insight to become aware of the tremendous impact we have during even the most brief encounter with people going through significant emotional events, and will offer tools for scene compassion without becoming "too wrapped up in someone else's emotions." On the contrary, you will come away from even the most tragic scene with the knowledge and sense that you did the right thing.

Develop Your Compassion

Nothing helps us build our perspective more than developing compassion for others. Compassion is a sympathetic feeling. It involves the willingness to put yourself in someone else's shoes, to take the focus off yourself and to imagine what it's like to be in someone else's predicament, and simultaneously, to feel love for that person. It's the recognition that other people's problems, their pain and frustrations, are every bit as real as our own - often far worse. In recognizing this fact and trying to offer some assistance, we open our hearts and greatly enhance our sense of gratitude.

Compassion is something you can develop with practice. It involves two things: intention and action. Intention simply means you remember to open your heart to others; you expand what and who matters, from yourself to other people. Action is simply the "what you do about it...."

Compassion develops your sense of gratitude by taking your attention off all the little things that most of us have learned to take too seriously. When you take time, often to reflect on the miracle of life...the gift of sight, of love, and all the rest, it can help to remind you that many of the things that you think of as "big stuff" are really just "small stuff" that you are turning into big stuff.

Richard Carlson, Ph.D.

(Carlson, 1997, p.17,18)

Chapter 1: Understanding The Crisis Response

"Everything can be taken from a man but one thing: the last of the human freedoms - to choose one's own attitude in any given set of circumstances..."

Viktor Frankl

For emergency workers to appropriately deal with people in a state of crisis and to understand their needs, it is important to have a basic knowledge of the normal or usual range of behaviors before, during and after a powerful emotional situation. This chapter relies substantially on the information generated by Dr. Jeffrey T. Mitchell, a former paramedic and firefighter who now serves as the President of the International Critical Incident Stress Foundation. Much of this material was published in a different form in the book, *Emergency Response to Crisis* (Mitchell and Resnik, 1986). It is used here with permission.

Prior to Emotional Crisis

People typically go through everyday life in a "steady state." This "state" is a balance between the mental systems of thoughts and emotions. Hold your arms straight out from your body and make a teeter-totter. Imagine the left arm is your thinking side and your right arm is your emotions, and like a teeter-totter, as one side goes up the other down. As we go through each day we have ups and downs. If someone cuts you off on the freeway, your emotional side goes up and you may say or do things without thinking. While working an emergency call, thinking and concentration go up, you focus on the task at hand (auto-pilot) pushing emotions down.

What is a Crisis?

This "steady state" between the thought and emotional systems fluctuates as we go through each day. Some experiences are more emotional than others, but in general, unless the situations we experience are very stressful, thinking predominates over feeling and thoughtful or emotional states remain somewhat balanced. Any serious interruption in this balance is considered a crisis. A crisis is best defined as an acute reaction to a demand (critical incident) in which three conditions are present. The conditions are:

1) The "steady state" between thinking and emotions is disrupted
2) Usual coping methods fail in the face of the demand
3) There is evidence of impairment in those who are experiencing the event. Impairment can be mild, moderate or severe. An example of mild impairment is a person forgeting a phone number that he or she usually dials from memory many times a day. Severe impairment is apparent when a person completely "freezes up" and is unable to take appropriate action in response to an overwhelming demand.

When the steady state is disrupted the emotional side of the balance overpowers the thinking side of the balance. Decision-making, planning and initiating action become more difficult. Anxiety, fear, sadness, anger, guilt, shock and feelings of terror predominate. In some circumstances, strong emotional outbursts replace effective action. It is safe to say that overall human performance deteriorates as emotions escalate.

A crisis, by the way, is a very personal thing. It is important to note that a crisis is always real to the person experiencing it. What may not seem like a big deal to you or me may be very significant to the person who has just called 9-1-1.

Crisis Characteristics

Typically, the emotional crises that emergency workers encounter have common characteristics. Four distinguishing features of crisis have been identified and they should be implemented into emergency worker thinking to assist in managing on-scene emotional trauma.

1. Crises are sudden. Traumatic injuries, crime situations and sudden medical emergencies are usually the case. When someone calls 9-1-1, you can expect that this crisis has suddenly erupted into a situation that requires your assistance

2. Because a crisis is sudden, the person is not adequately prepared to handle the situation (emotions over-ride thinking) and his or her coping mechanisms are not working very well.

3. Crises are short in duration. The crises emergency personnel deal with are happening *NOW*. In some cases death occurs while we are still on the scene.

4. Crises have the potential to produce dangerous or unacceptable behavior.

Remember, as the emotional side gets out of control, the thinking side gets pushed down. People undergoing a significant crisis may say and do things without thinking clearly.

"Emergency service personnel need a working knowledge of the effects of severe stress and crisis on the average person. Without this knowledge, they are prone to underestimate their critical role in managing crisis. The assistance provided by emergency service personnel has deep and lasting effects upon the victims"

(Mitchell & Resnik, 1986, p. 5).

Crisis Phases

Research in the field of grief supports the concept that most people pass through somewhat predictable phases of grief when they encounter the death of a relative or a friend. They also experience certain emotional stages if they have been diagnosed with a terminal illness. Shock, denial, anger, bargaining and reconciliation are some of the typical stages people experience when encountering their own mortality. Likewise, people take a similar predictable path when going through sudden emotional crisis. The following stages represent the usual pattern of emotional reactions during a crisis.

1. High Anxiety
2. Denial
3. Anger
4. Remorse
5. Grief
6. Reconciliation

* **High Anxiety or Emotional Shock.** This is the initial reaction to the crisis. People will deal with their crises in very different ways. It is important to note that people in this phase can either be bouncing off the walls or sitting and doing nothing. They have had no time to prepare emotionally for their sudden crisis. So much is happening so fast that the brain is unable to comprehend. "Death does not make sense; the mind cannot comprehend or absorb the meaning" (Redmond, 1996, p. 54).

A young single father sat on the couch as emergency workers desperately tried to revive his SIDS afflicted baby. He sat there emotionless in a state of emotional shock. Unfortunately, this "non-activity" was perceived as uncaring and caused an initial investigation of child abuse against him. This young father not only lost his child, but was put through interrogation because of a misinterpretation of his lack of response during the resuscitation attempts. In some circumstances we think people are handling the situation very well and even thank them for their understanding, when in fact they are in emotional shock. "One of the saddest parts of trauma is that people assume you are strong when you really are in shock" (Lord, 1994, p. 19).

* **Denial.** Denial is the brain's way of protecting us from too much stressful input that comes too fast. Elizabeth Kuebler-Ross, in her book *On Death and Dying,* explains denial as a "buffer after unexpected shocking news, that allows the person time to collect themselves and, with time, mobilize other, less radical defenses" (1997, p. 52). It is not uncommon to hear family members telling each other that everything will be okay while we are working on their loved one, regardless of the seriousness of the injuries.

* **Anger.** Anger is a normal response to frustration. When denial can no longer buffer the stressful input, anger may replace it. It is important to remember that for these folks, their world is coming apart. Their loved one is seriously ill or dead. They are functioning on heightened emotions and the situation is changing rapidly. Strangers are often present in what would usually be their private comfort zone. You can imagine their feelings of helplessness. They become overwhelmed and frustrated by the situation. Sometimes they express anger at their loved one or even you. Be careful not to take their anger personally. Anger is simply a natural reaction to fear and frustration.

These first three phases of the emotional reaction to crisis, which frequently arise in the first few hours after exposure to a critical event, are followed by other stages of emotional reaction including remorse, grief and reconciliation. The experience of the first three emotional reactions in a crisis response, however, sets the stage for people to proceed through the remaining emotions. Complications in the first few phases almost always assure problems in the latter phases of the crisis response and the subsequent grief process because people can get stuck in shock, denial and anger.

The first three phases are the typical phases in which emergency workers are going to encounter people in a crisis state. The early phases, shock, denial and anger are those in which people are most vulnerable to psychological harm. It is interesting to note that people in those same early stages of a crisis response are also "vulnerable" or open to help. "Assistance provided by public safety personnel during the first one to three hours of the crisis is often more significant in terms of the overall crisis than much of the help which is provided by hospital staff and counselors" (Mitchell & Resnik, p. 5,6).

An analogy may help us to gain an understanding of why the first three phases of a crisis are so important. Let's say we walk around with a force field surrounding us. It repels most of the minor disturbances that we encounter. During a significant emotional event, this force field is removed, your chest is "cut open," and your ribs spread to expose your "inner being." This vulnerable inner being acts like a photo negative that allows exposure during the length

4

of these first three phases. Everything that is seen, heard, felt, smelled and said is permanently "photographed" by the individual undergoing crisis. Later, when the individual has reconciled him or herself to the loss, these vivid photographs can and will surface. Research evidence in the field of loss and grief indicates that virtually everyone over the age of reason and of sound mind will remember exactly how they were informed of the death of a loved one and how others treated them during their crisis response. That is why it is critical to understand and treat these survivors with care and concern. Survivors will remember everything you do and say while you are with them.

In my case, for example, I can remember virtually every second from the moment the Fire Chief showed up at my house to tell me there had been an accident and that my young son, Justin, had drowned, to leaving the hospital 24 hours later. In this window of time, everything that was said, done, felt, or heard is permanently imprinted inside of me. And of course, my wife has the horrible imprint of the emergency scene itself and the awful impression made by the emergency personnel who blocked her from holding Justin. What kind of impression did you leave at your last death scene?

* **Remorse.** This emotional phase of a reaction to a crisis is filled with feelings of sadness and guilt. The shock of the earlier stages in the crisis response begins to slacken and the overwhelming feelings of loss and grief become more apparent. It is rare for this phase to begin early in a crisis response. Most people need some time to sort out the experience of the loss before they feel the intensity of this phase. Sadness becomes pervasive and the survivors begin to feel that they should have or could have done something to prevent the loss of the friend or family member. Even well after the fact of a death has been established, people may fantasize about doing something that could undo the loss or "rewind the tape" so that the tragedy could be prevented.

* **Grief.** The process of grieving over the loss of a loved one has its origins, of course, while one is still struggling with the state of shock and high anxiety that is associated with encountering the bad news. The deepest aspects of grief, however, are not processed while a person is in a state of shock. True grief does not usually appear until several weeks after the loss. Then people become more fully aware of the loss they have experienced. Over time they work though the meaning of the relationship they had with the deceased and find a new orientation to their lives. Going through all of the steps associated with a grief reaction can take a long period of time. It is, therefore, rare to see some one in grief in the early stages of crisis response unless they are suffering from the depression of a previous loss when the shock of a new loss has occurred.

* **Reconciliation.** No one is ever happy over the loss of a loved one. As time passes, however, a person passes gradually through a series of stages of grief. The loss becomes somewhat

easier to bare. Life may take on new joys and excitement. The deceased becomes the focus of an important memory, but the bereaved are gradually able to find a sense of hope and renewal that was absent during the most intense phases of the grief process.

It is important enough to be stated again here. Insensitive or poorly informed people who are involved in the care of a person in the first few phases of a crisis response may produce lasting negative impressions that ultimately interfere with the survivors ability to reach the state of reconciliation described above. What kind of an impression do you wish to make the next time you have to manage a scene in which a death has occurred?

Chapter 2: Responsibilities of Emergency Responders

"Caring for the dying makes you poignantly aware not only of their mortality, but also of your own...To feel the full force of your mortality, and to open your heart entirely to it, is to allow to grow in you that all-encompassing, fearless compassion that fuels the lives of all those who wish truly to be of help to others."

Sogyal Rinpoche
(1993, p. 187)

Remember, our actions, our words, the sights and sounds of the scene, stay with the surviving family members forever. That fact, of course, intensifies the stress on us as individuals who have a responsibility to keep an already tragic scene from getting worse. We do not want to be in the position of not handling the survivors very well. There is a lot of pressure on emergency workers to do the right thing. "In general, the mistaken approach (by emergency responders) assumes that people need to be protected: to be told indirectly, to not be allowed to see the body, and be told platitudes about loss" (Barrett, 1995).

There are two ways to deal with the added stresses connected with significant others at the scene. Emergency workers can be callused. They can put up the fire line or police tape, and keep everyone away. Then they can limit their contact with the victims or survivors of an incident and tell them as little as possible. The other method of dealing with survivors is to be compassionate. To be compassionate means that a person understands emotional crisis, and takes a few simple actions and speaks some caring words.

I will never forget the very first time I took the compassionate route at an emergency scene. I remember not because of the stress it inflicted, but because of the sense of peace I found in doing the right thing. It was a cold January afternoon. The sun was shining and the air crisp. A beautiful day! The young eighteen year-old girl had just finished lunch with her parents and left for work in her shiny new sports car. As she traveled over a hill in the roadway, an oncoming pickup truck appeared in her lane. It was too late for either driver to react.

The rescue, engine and ambulance arrived. The impact was severe. The young girl, still safely belted in her seat was unconscious with agonal respirations. We carefully removed the young lady from her vehicle and placed

7

her on the ground. She was not breathing now; her pupils were dilated and unresponsive, and her EKG showed a heart rhythm that was not encouraging. Basic and advanced life support was initiated while an emergency room physician was consulted over a cell-phone. We were not in an area accessible by helicopter or rapid ground transportation. As the young girl's heart slowly stopped beating, the doctor gave the orders to discontinue resuscitation efforts.

At that same moment, we looked up and saw an older man and woman rapidly approaching on foot, with a young boy and girl close behind. It was the girl's parents, younger brother and sister. The parents recognized the car and they recognized the clothing. They were intercepted about 50 feet from their daughter's car. We told them to stay there just for a minute. The on-scene police officers were briefed on what our intentions were, and consulted to make sure it was all right for the parents to come into the scene. We went back to the parents and informed them the condition of their daughter; the blood, the emergency medical equipment still attached. But we let them know that if they wanted to be with her, we would stay by their side. We walked up to the body together. Blankets were brought out, and as the mother wept and held her daughter's hand, the dad tucked in his child for the last time. Blankets were given to the brother and sister to keep them warm as we answered questions about the death as best we could.

Was this difficult? Yes it was. But how much more difficult would it have been to struggle with the family to keep them away? Chaplains were dispatched to the scene to continue family support when the fire apparatus left. Back in the fire station, I felt a sense of relief instead of anxiety, knowing we had done the right thing. We had taken a scene of tragedy and made it a scene of caring. All the agencies there, police, fire and ambulance, commented how well this difficult situation played out.

What We Can Do

---

1. **Be Truthful**
2. **Dose Out the Bad News**
3. **Allow Significant Others to Spend Time with Their Loved One**
4. **Convey Caring**
5. **Allow Grief**
6. **Offer Continued Support**

At scenes of sudden death we can't always change what happened, but we can always leave an impression that we cared. When we do things properly, the situation does not change for the grieving survivors. They may draw some small comfort from our actions, but only much later after the event has passed. When we do things poorly, however, our incompetence remains with them forever.

1.Be Truthful

Surviving family members, during times of emotional crisis, will have many questions that should be answered truthfully. A woman shared with me how, years ago, she received the dreaded 3 A.M. knock on the door. A gentleman, identifying himself as a fire department chaplain, told her there had been a terrible accident involving her daughter, and that her daughter had died. Later that morning the police showed up at her home. As they began asking her questions about the daughter, it became apparent that this was not an accident. Her daughter had been shot and killed by her boyfriend. In this mom's mind, the chaplain had lied. This was a brutal murder! As she reflected on this incident, she again became visibly angry. In defense of the chaplain, and all of us who do not know quite what to say in situations like this, he most probably was trying to make the news easier on the mom as well as himself. But, it was the wrong thing to say, leaving a lasting impression of ineptitude and a lack of caring. What could have been said? He could have said something to the effect of "I'm sorry but something tragic has happened; your daughter has been shot, and has died." Not quite the whole story, but not a lie. The chaplain then could have sat with her and answered truthfully any question the mom had regarding the incident as she was ready to ask them.

When significant others show up at the scene they may have questions. "Did they suffer?" "Were their eyes open?" " Was is fast?" etc. are crucial questions to them and need to be answered truthfully.

2. "Dose out" the Bad News

The shock of bad news is a jolt to the emotional, intellectual and physical components of a human being. Our systems are designed to withstand enormous stress. Extremely high levels of stress, however, typically produce disruption and possible damage to our systems. To keep the mind, body and emotions from being overwhelmed, bad news should be "dosed out." Giving painful news in measured doses helps the person hearing it to adjust to it and to sustain the least amount of psychological and physical damage. Here is an example of "dosing out" a painful announcement.

a) Mr. and / or Mrs. _____. I am _____ with the _____ (organization). May I come in and sit down with you. I have some very important information to share with you.
b) I am afraid I have some very bad news for you. It is difficult for me to tell you this information, but it must be done. Just a few minutes ago I was asked to come to your home to personally relate this news.
c) There was an accident this evening involving your daughter, who was a passenger in her friend's car.
d) The accident was a very serious one.
e) In fact, the accident involved a fatality.
f) It is very painful for me to tell you this, but I must, unfortunately, inform you that your daughter was critically injured in that accident.
e) She was unconscious at the scene and flown off site by med-evac helicopter.
e) Your daughter was treated at _____ hospital.
f) Despite all efforts of the medical staff, your daughter was declared dead just a short time ago. I came immediately to your home once

she was identified as your daughter and it became certain that you were, in fact, her family.
g) I am so sorry for the pain this terrible news causes you.
h) I will stay with you to assist you as much as I can in contacting some of your own resources.

Each piece of information should be followed by a brief pause long enough to monitor the faces of those who are receiving it. If they appear ready to hear the next piece of information, proceed. If unsure, the presenter should gently ask if the family members are ready for the presenter to move ahead. Do not rush the death announcement, but do not drag it out either. Too fast is brutal and does not give people time to properly adjust to the turmoil produced by the news. An announcement that is too slow is torture to the survivors and produces undo pain.

Death announcements should be made face-to-face and not by phone. They should also be in private. A team approach is usually quite helpful whenever that is possible. Make sure the person's name is used to assure that no mistakes are made regarding the identity of the deceased. It is also important to make sure that those who hear the news are told how the death occurred.

As many facts as possible should be known by the presenter before the contact is made. The words "dead," "death," "died," or "fatal" should be used in the announcement. When people ask questions, they are usually ready for additional information. If some of the details are gruesome, they may be held until later; or the recipient might be asked how much they really want to know right now. If a recipient of bad news is in fragile health, a decision is usually made to hold back the most gruesome aspects of the announcement until the person's medical doctor can be consulted for advice. When giving the details of a death to a loved one in fragile health, the necessity to slow it down and make sure small doses are used is crucial. Make sure there is another family member or close friend with the person as the news is given. There have been some cases in which news of a horrific nature, which could upset a delicate person, was given with an ambulance standing by.

It is important to make sure that the existence of other resources or sources of information are offered to the family members. The one making the death announcement should leave a card or information on how to contact that person again in case there are lingering questions.

3. Allow Significant Others to Spend Time With Their Loved One

Allowing people to spend time with their loved one conjures up all sorts of emotions. It is time to put your own thoughts about this aside and do what is right. People who are allowed to spend time with their loved one at the time of death do better emotionally in the long run. When a family member shows up at an emergency scene where their loved one is seriously injured or dead, they should be given the choice of what they want to do. If the patient is still alive and being worked on, the family member should be allowed to be near as long as they do not interfere. Most of the actions of the emergency personnel, including emergency medical care, should be explained to them. This not only helps the family members to understand everything that is being done, but it also helps them to realize that kind and concerned people are caring for the patient. In some situations, the patient hears the information and is reassured as well. The patients usually find comfort in having their relatives near by.

At the scenes of serious injuries or fatalities, a systematic approach is helpful to mitigate potential problems that may occur when dealing with distraught significant others. Here are some suggestions:

A. **Close family members and significant others need to be identified and separated from other on-lookers.** These significant others" become your VIPs. When safe to do so, they are allowed inside the security of the scene where someone explains to them the situation and answers their questions. In some situations, it has been necessary to ask those who want to get close to the scene to identify themselves or to have known family members vouch for them.

B. **If there is a fatality, tell the VIPs truthfully that their loved one has died and give them the choice to be with the body.** Approximately 99.9% of the time they will want to be with the body (it is still their loved one). Have someone from the emergency services stay nearby them for support if they decide to be with the body.

C. **Explain to them what they will see.** Be honest. If there is blood, disfigurement, or other abnormal sights, tell the family, and again give them the choice to be with the body. "Survivors should be allowed to make a choice about seeing, touching, or holding the body of their loved one. Those who are in a position to assist a family at a scene should be very clear in describing the condition of the body, so the choice is an informed one" (Lord, p. 8). I have found that no matter what the situation is, the body is still their loved one.

A lady explained to me that her son had been murdered and his body was not discovered for several weeks. Because of body's advanced decomposition, the coroner did not allow her to see her son's body in the morgue. After a year of struggling, she was able to see the pictures of the scene. "I had pictured it much worse in my mind" she told me. "I wish they would have let me be with him." For a year, this woman had lived without closure. Scenes like this will be rare for field operations personnel, but it is important for us to understand the need of people to be with their deceased loved one.

One thing that has worked for me when I have had to assist family members who wish to view a disfigured body is to keep the body covered with a blanket, and let the family uncover small areas of the body when they want to see them. This procedure helps people to keep the viewing of bodies of

11

deceased relatives and/ or friends under their own control.

D. **Stay With the Relatives or Friends.** Chaplains are great with this. However, if chaplain services are not yet available at the scene, this may be up to the emergency responders. Each situation is different. Sometimes it is appropriate to stay next to the grieving relative. Sometimes it is more appropriate to stay in the background.

4. Convey Caring

"People don't care how much you know, until they know how much you care." We can't always change the outcome of a tragedy or ease the profound pain survivors may be going through, but we can imprint a lasting memory that someone cares about what is happening. I can assure you that these people will remember the kindness in their reflection of the event.

I'll always remember my pager going off while I was off-duty on a Christmas morning. It was a request to respond to a fatal motor vehicle accident. An 18 year-old girl, on her way to church in her new Christmas dress, hit an icy spot on the road and lost control. Her car hit a tree, killing her instantly. Her younger brother, also in the car, survived with minor injuries. The emergency responders on the scene recognized two things: first, that this Christmas morning tragedy had the propensity to produce critical incident stress among themselves, and second, that the rest of the family, also on their way to church, was arriving on the scene. Because I lecture to these responders about dealing with families, they called for me to respond.

Upon arrival, I found the "VIPs" had already been separated from the rest of the gathered crowd. A firefighter was standing with them explaining that their daughter had died and that someone was on their way to assist them. The Incident Commander was explaining to the on-scene police agency the importance of the family being with their loved one, and the fact that the Fire District had a program to assist them (the family) in doing so. I met with the medics on the scene and inquired about the condition of the body (I did not need to physically see it). I then explained to the family what their daughter's visual condition was and told them that if they would like to be with her, we would go with them.

The daughter had a massive head injury, but to the family she was so beautiful in her new Christmas dress. The mother gently uncovered her daughter, wept, and gave her a hug. The family then gently covered her back up, tucking in the sides of the blanket to keep her warm. The firefighters at this scene had recognized the situation and they had understood that they might be not be able to deal with it properly themselves. Requesting help when you are feeling overwhelmed is very appropriate.

I met the family again more a year after this incident. They approached me and identified themselves. They remembered what had been done at the scene and thanked us for caring. If this isn't what we are in the business for, I don't know what is.

I have found that family members share common concerns for their deceased loved one.

> * They want to be with the body before it gets cold.
> * They want to make the body comfortable.
> * They want to say good-bye where the death happened.
> * They want to resolve any conflicts they may have had with the deceased.

5. Allow Grief

Everyone expresses their grief in a different way. Allow people to express themselves in their own way, without interference. The exceptions to this rule of thumb would be in cases where there is destructive or unlawful behavior. In those circumstances, people should be warned that the behavior is unacceptable and that the police will be brought in if they do not cease the destructive or unlawful behavior. Try to understand the phases of emotional crisis that were described in the first chapter. Understand that frustration may lead to anger. Some anger may be aimed the emergency workers. Operations personnel should be warned not to take anger personally. Allow the significant others to validate their loss and to participate in activities that foster closure.

6. Offer Continued Support

Assess the needs of the situation. Develop a sector under the Incident Command system to take care of survivors. In my community, we assign an "Occupant Services" sector (or group under the National Incident Management System) on all incidents in which someone is undergoing crisis. It does not matter whether their crisis reaction is due to a fire, an accident or any other situation, This sector's sole function is to take care of our "VIPs." Chaplains work very well in this capacity, but firefighters can also be trained in crisis intervention and have demonstrated their abilities in many areas of the country. The crisis intervener sits with the bereaved and makes sure that the survivors' needs are taken care of and their questions are answered. They make sure the survivor, or "occupant", is not left alone. It is a good idea to develop a "prompt sheet" that is compatible with current incident check lists to help assist those providing crisis intervention services to begin their communications with distraught people at the scenes of tragedies.

Covering the body

Covering the body shows respect of privacy for the deceased and their family. Just remember, when you cover a body, try to cover the entire body. Most times those yellow emergency blankets that are carried on fire, rescue and law enforcement vehicles across the country will not be large enough to cover the entire body when adults are involved. Get in the habit of paying attention to this and, if needed, use two blankets. Family members can often identify a deceased family member by some article of clothing like their shoes or pants. If they have this recognition before the emergency personnel can properly inform them of the death of their loved one, they may suffer more from the shock of such a recognition than they would have in the case of a proper notification. Also keep in mind that survivors are concerned about the comfort and protection of their loved one even in death. Some are very concerned about the loved one getting cold on the scene. Having the top of the head or the feet sticking out from under the covering does not help to protect the family members and friends from additional anguish over the death of a loved one.

In outdoor deaths, such as car accidents or sporting activities, after the body is covered, take a tarp and cover the entire car if possible. This helps keep the "gawkers" from bothering you, plus it gives the family an insulation layer in their brief journey to their loved one. In inclement weather, the additional tarp expresses that you care about their loved one's comfort and the condition of their body.

In situations involving in-home deaths, I typically ask the family if they have a blanket with which they would like the loved one covered. The yellow emergency blankets scream out "hey, there is a body here!". I will also ask the family if they want the head covered. Remember, comfort is a vital issue with survivors, and a covered head may not look natural or comfortable to them.

Conclusion

Crisis intervention at a death scene is neither expensive nor is it complicated. A kind, careful and gentle approach to managing the dead at the scene will do much to assist the bereaved. Showing respect and compassion, providing adequate information, guidance and access to the body of a loved one are kindnesses which will always be remembered long after the burial of a loved person.

Chapter 3: Kind Words & Caring Actions

"A good death notification and nothing changes...A bad death notification and everything changes"

Parent of murdered child

When my son was in the hospital (he was on a ventilator for 24 hours), a hospital chaplain asked if he could pray with us. He stood over my son's bed and prayed that if he (my son) "would not be whole again, Lord, please take him." At the time I thought it was a pretty stupid thing to say because I wanted Justin to live, whole or not. My wife and I would have taken him home regardless of the mental status, breathing tubes and IV lines, but I was still in the initial phase of my emotional shock and had other things on my mind. I let the prayer pass without much of a reaction. Later when it was decided Justin was not going to recover, the chaplain again prayed over him for God "to take him if he is not whole." Internally, I became angry. It was obvious that this man did not have children of his own. The prayer was not well thought out. No matter how well-meaning the prayer was, it was not helpful and caused pain.

In hindsight I began to feel somewhat sorry for the chaplain. I could imagine the frustration he must have felt in dealing with the parents of a dying child. Obviously, no one taught him how to pray at times like this.

In reflecting on the calls I've been on, I am embarrassed by some of the things I have said to people when they were undergoing emotional crisis. When they were most vulnerable and when everything said and done was permanently imprinted in them, my words were not helpful. But nobody told me what to say either.

Lois Chapman Dick describes how people "think they must stop the person who has been traumatized from feeling bad, so they say things they hope will stop their pain." When we tell the grieving that their loved one is "no longer in pain", or "in a better place," they hear "shut up, stop grieving," and "stop feeling what you are feeling" (1996, p. 180). The following statements are things said and heard at emergency scenes that should never have been said.

Never Say

"I know how you feel," That is impossible unless you have been

there. Unless you have had a child drown at the baby-sitters, you don't know how I felt. Unless you've lost your spouse of 50 years, you can not know what the person who has is feeling. I was sitting with a friend of mine who had just lost his infant daughter in a car accident. We were at the reception following the funeral. Another friend came up to the dad and stated "I know how you feel, I've got children too." Although the grieving dad said "thank you," I couldn't help but think how absurd this sounded.

*"*I understand.*" Most of the time you do not. Again, it is impossible to know the history the loved ones had with each other.

* "*You shouldn't feel that way.*" People have the right to feel the way they do. Feelings cannot be changed by a directive to feel otherwise. Anyway they look at it, their world has been turned up-side-down. Allow the survivors to express their feelings.

*"*You're so strong.*" A person in high anxiety may be in a non-active state. When they begin to reconcile their grief, they will remember this statement and think you are an "idiot". What does "strong" have to do with being in emotional pain? People never feel strong when they are grieving.

*"*You must get on with your life.*" Who are we as emergency responders to tell anyone to get on with their life? Grief takes time. Nobody is past their grief until they have passed through their grief. That process can take months or years depending on the circumstances. Some will never finish their grief process in the course of their lifetime.

*"*You'll get over it.*" No one "gets over" a tragedy. At best, survivors learn to cope with what has happened. "Getting over it" may also imply that you want them to forget about their loved one. Again, such a comment asks people to do the impossible.

* "*If you only had...*" Sometimes the circumstances leading to tragedy are so obvious, emergency responders want to lecture the survivors. The husband's acute chest pain that started 4 hours prior to the 9-1-1 call, the unrestrained driver, the guns laying around the house, the kids riding bicycles without helmets, all can bring frustration and anger to those trying to save these people's lives. Believe me, the significant others will dwell on these tragic circumstances all by themselves without our help.

*"*Your anguish won't bring them back.*" This comment states the obvious and people generally resent that. Such a comment generates nothing except anger. Again, let the survivor deal with the crisis in their own way. They know their loved one will not be coming back.

Why rub salt in the wound?

*"*They led a good life.*"*   This statement is not much of a consolation when someone has a big gaping hole in their life where a person used to be.   Maybe they did lead a "good life" but most probably the survivor was not yet ready to give them up.

*"*Do not question God's will.*"*   Some theologians will argue it is not God's will to have people die.   There are many beliefs, and various religions understand death differently.   Bringing divine meaning to anything tragic during emotional crisis may only add confusion and frustration.   The survivor will have plenty of time after the crisis to reflect on the purpose and put meaning to the situation. "This consolation (It was Gods will) may cause more pain to victim families than any other well-intended phrase.   A sudden, violent death is absurd. Your loved one didn't deserve it. You don't deserve it.   Therefore, for God to have willed it makes no sense" (Lord, p. 104).

*"*You'll find someone else.*"*   Looking to the future is not what survivors want to think about.   You do not understand, nor are expected to understand, the history of any relationship other than your own. Many people are very much in love and satisfied with their relationships and do not want to think of life without their loved one.

*"*Be thankful you have other children.*"*   When Justin died, I canceled a speaking engagement for the local Senior Citizen group. When I went back after some time off, I sat down with Ann (not her real name), the elderly woman who scheduled the get-to-gethers. I told her why I had canceled. Ann asked me if I had other children. When I told her I had one other son she shared that she had raised five children. When they were young, the middle boy died. She told me a friend came up to her after the death and said "be thankful you have other kids." Ann shared that she wanted five kids, not four, and that the middle one was just as loved and important as the others. Ann thought this remark insensitive and uncaring even after all these years.

*"*It would have been worse if...*"*   Resist the urge to make things seem "not as bad." To the person undergoing emotional crisis, it doesn't get any worse than the situation at hand. Such comments are always viewed as insensitive.

What to Say

I used to teach emergency responder's things to say at difficult times. I had a whole list of phrases presumed to bring comfort to those grieving and to make our job easier, but as I took a serious look at them, they seemed forced, corny and not genuine. Here is what generally works:

*It is okay to state that the situation is difficult for you as an
emergency services person.* In general, people truly respect the public
safety uniformed services. Imagine the sense of respect they feel when
a "hero" goes beyond the call of duty to share someone else's grief. I
had finished giving a presentation on fire safety to a group of adults
when an elderly gentleman approached me and took me aside. He
shared that the fire department had responded to his house years ago
when his wife passed away. He asked me if I knew what he remembered
most about the experience. I was puzzled. He went on to say that
when the medics stopped working on his wife, one of them came up to
him and shared how difficult it was to see someone else's loved one
die. He shared that it was a scene he would always remember, and
stated, "You guys really care about what happens, don't you?"

* *"I'm Sorry."*   There are probably no words easier to say or more
appropriate than "I'm Sorry."

Ask to hear about their loved one. I am a history buff. Once, when
sitting at the kitchen table with a grieving wife, trying to gather the needed
information for my incident report, I noticed a railroad retirement plaque on
the wall bearing the name of her just deceased husband. "I see your husband
retired from the railroad" I said. This seemed to create a spark in her, that
someone was interested in her husband's "story." I received a neat history
lesson on the railroad and her husband's work, and she received the feeling
that someone cared about her husband's life. After a person has been
declared dead at the scene (this works best in the comfort of their home),
take the time to ask "What did Bill (obviously use the name of the deceased!)
do for a living?" In most cases, they will be happy to share their memories.

A mother with her two children, while traveling on the freeway, lost
control of her car, went through the median strip and crashed underneath
the trailer of a semi-truck. The car then burst into flames. The mom and
her kids died instantly. A few days later, the sister of the deceased mom
came into my office to inquire about the deaths. Constant visions of her
sister and kids struggling and burning alive were in her head. I assured her
(because of witness and crew accounts) that her loved ones had most
probably died on impact. This seemed to provide some comfort. Later on
that day, the husband of the grieving sister came to see me. It was obvious
that, even though this couple hadnot been on the scene, the event had
caused them a great deal of emotional grief. For some reason, a letter to
these grieving people seemed appropriate to help them work through
theunimaginable scenes they were carrying. I have reprinted the essence
of the letter here in case it helps.

Dear Mr. & Mrs. _____

We would like to express our deepest sorrow to you for the loss of your sister and nieces. We appreciate both of your contacts with us and we did pass along your gratitude to the crews who responded to the accident. We know this is an extremely difficult time for your family, but hope you may find some comfort in knowing that Jennifer* and her children were treated with the utmost respect and care. We have found that our personnel deal with situations like this much better when they are allowed to express the same gentle and compassionate treatment to the victims as they would want for their own families . You can be assured that this practice was given to your sister and her kids.

Again, thank you for your contact with us. Our thoughts are with you.
Respectfully,
Capt. Tim W. Dietz

Sometimes Just Being There Helps

We tend to worry a great deal about what we should or should not say when dealing with the relatives and friends of a deceased person. But often it is a wordless gesture which means the most. Simple things, such as holding a door open, offering a chair or a respectful nod of the head, can assist the bereaved. In some circumstances attendance at the wake or funeral may be a consolation to family members.

Let Touch Convey Caring

Sometimes there are no words that can be said. A simple touch to the shoulder can say it all. There seems to be a comforting power in human touch that I can not explain. There were over 400 people at my son's funeral. Three of them touched me, and unknowingly left a bond that is everlasting and bears mentioning. As I bowed in a church bench, Jim, my captain at the time, and Sandee, an administrative secretary with my fire department, separately came by and put their hands over mine. I felt a great sense of compassion. Outside the church, Doug, with whom I used to dig drain fields, gave me a hug. I explain this because, after more than 14 years, the power of these simple actions is still deeply imprinted on my "photograph" of that emotional event and provides comfort yet today.

Getting "touchy-feely" is not typically in an emergency worker's tool box. These words and actions can be accomplished without getting emotionally involved with the bereaved. You can show compassion without shouldering it, and the emotional benefit you leave and receive far outweigh the fear of taking a caring action.

* Not her real name

Chapter 4: Difficult Situations

"Let us not be content to wait and see what will happen, but give us the determination to make the right things happen"

Peter Marshall

In the emergency services, nothing remains constant. Just when you think you have seen it all, you are faced with a new challenge. The following situations can throw quirks into emergency scene compassion if you're not prepared to handle them.

Grossly Disfigured Bodies

This was also addressed in the chapter on responsibilities of emergency workers. Just what do we let civilians see? Remember, survivors want and need to be with their loved one at the time of death. If not allowed to see the body, they typically will imagine things much worse than they really are. The following rules will assist in dealing with this difficult scenario:

* **Always be truthful about the situation.** Remember, when the survivors come out of their shock of the situation, they will remember everything you said to them. If you lied about something, when they find out they will become extremely angry and disappointed with you.

* **Give them the choice of whether or not to be with the deceased.** Let them make the decision. As stated in Chapter 2, clearly describe the condition of the body and what will be seen so that survivors can make an informed choice about being with their loved one. The body should be covered and shielded from the general public. After the explanation of the deceased's condition, allow the significant other to uncover it as they are ready.

* **Explain what they will see.** If I'm not the one who dealt directly with the body, I do not particularly need to see it. I will ask the initial responder what the deceased looks like, and then relay that to the family.

* **Have one family member look and let them help decide if the rest of the family should see.** I was summoned to the scene of an eighteen year-old boy who had died in a car accident. The boy's brothers and parents were on the scene. The mother desperately wanted to be with her son, but there was concern because of her inability to walk due to the profound grief. One of the older sons looked at the deceased brother, and then convinced the mom that she should wait until her child was taken to the mortuary. The bereaved mother seemed to accept this from him.

If there is a question of allowing significant others to be with grossly disfigured loved ones, it may be helpful to have a single family member be an advocate between you and the family. Allow them to look and help decide the course of action.

* **Have someone stay with them.** Do not leave these folks alone. Someone needs to stay with them. It doesn't matter if this is a representative from the fire department, police department or the coroner's office. If time permits, get a trained chaplain to the scene to be with the family.

* **You do not need to look at the body with them.** Emergency responders will see their share of bodies. Typically, I'll stay with the survivor and look at something else while they are saying good-bye. It is possible to show compassion and caring and still "detach" yourself from the situation.

* **It does not need to be you.** There may come a situation that hits "too close to home," and brings up past or present personal stressors. If you feel uncomfortable dealing with a particular situation, it is normal and okay. The important thing is that you recognize the need. Call for support services, such as a chaplain trained in this, or another responder who is willing and able. There may be times when the body is in such bad condition that it may be unidentifiable. In these cases, it is best that the family be told of this and suggest that identification be delayed until the coroner's office is on the scene or until the body is at the mortuary.

Emergency Equipment on the Body

Leaving medical paraphernalia on the body was something we always did. There was never a question about leaving our equipment in place after a death was called. Families saw intubation tubes, EKG patches and, occasionally, I.V. lines still in place. I always assumed the medical examiner wanted it that way. What kind of "final imprint" does this leave in the survivor's mind? Finally we consulted our County medical examiner to question this practice. The advice was "unless homicide is suspected, remove your equipment." I would suggest you consult with your local medical examiner's office and see what its policy is.

A concern was raised to me: "Won't the family question whether or not we really tried if they don't see any indication of equipment laying around?" Again, every situation is different. But if the resuscitation efforts are explained to the "VIPs" then this should not be a concern.

When We Can't Let People into the Scene

There will be times when it is inappropriate or unsafe for relatives to be allowed with their loved ones. During these situations, remember to set up an area for the "VIPs" with an emergency services representative to explain what the situation is.

* **Crime Scenes.** Obviously, the less folks allowed into a crime scene, the better it is for the investigators. Typically, emergency responders can retrace their steps at the scene when interviewed. Emotionally

distraught relatives may not be able to do so. Remember as well that alcohol related motor vehicle accidents may also be considered crime scenes. When in doubt, ask the police agency on scene if it is okay for relatives to be with their loved one. It is important that all agencies working an emergency scene know the significance of allowing scene compassion. In motor vehicle crashes, when there is a possibility of crime involvement, officers should be able to allow controlled family entrance into the scene. Fully explain the situation to the family and let them know that disturbing the scene cannot be allowed. Always assign someone to stay with the bereaved.

* Mass Casualty Incidents. In emergency services, the survival of the sick and injured is the number one priority. In multiple patient scenarios, there is an organized confusion that takes place. Triage, treatment and transportation zones are established, and patient documentation and control are essential for the success of the scene. If relatives show up at these scenes, they must be kept from involvement to avoid any confusion regarding who is involved and who is not. These "VIPs" should be taken to the "VIP" area where an emergency services representative explains everything that is going on from the reason for distancing from the scene to treatment and transportation operations.

* Dangerous Environment. The very nature of emergency services work can involve or create dangerous environments. A good rule-of-thumb is that anytime emergency responders need to be in protective clothing, civilians can't be allowed into the area. This includes, but is not limited to:

> * Extrications
> * Hazardous materials incidents
> * Technical rescue situations; i.e. water, high angle, trench, confined space, etc.

In these situations, "VIPs" should be identified and taken to an area near the scene, but in a safe zone.

* Relatives Interfere with Resuscitation or Scene Control. Unfortunately, even with the best intentions, things don't always go as desired. In some cases, when survivors are in their "high anxiety" or "shock" stage of emotional crisis or display anger to the responders, they can become out of control. Their feelings may take total control of their thinking, and they may hinder resuscitation attempts or create an unsafe condition for themselves or the rescuers. In these instances, the "VIPs" will need to be restrained and taken from the scene. Stay with them, and once they are a safe distance away, a calm explanation of the situation may be helpful. Explain why they are being kept at a distance. Be honest. They will understand your caring concerns in their reflection on the incident.

Body Removals

Occasionally there are situations in which "doing the right thing" is based upon personal reasons. More times than I wish to remember, my crew had to respond to car accidents to extricate bodies from the wreckage after the medical examiner was through with the scene investigation. I do not particularly enjoy this and have found simple tools to help ease the situation, as well as the mind.

* **Treat every body with respect.** It doesn't matter if it's a single fatality or a plane crash with multiple deceased. Treat each body as you would want your most beloved family member to be treated. Responders at multiple death scenes will have more difficulty than normal if they are expected to "pick up the pieces," rather than removing human remains with respect.

* **Keep the body covered.** To help protect yourself in the situation, keep the body covered. I do not wish to have any memories of exposed body parts. Keep the body covered during extrication and removal. When possible, I will free the body and then have the coroner's office remove it. If you are put in the position of removal, keep the body wrapped in a blanket and treat it with respect. One particular incident comes to mind. We had to respond to a fatal accident scene to extricate and remove a young mother and her two children from a car. We kept all three victims tightly covered during the extrication and removal. Each person was carefully removed as if they were very fragile and then placed on a tarp. We were feeling that things had gone pretty well until an investigating officer had one of the firefighters hold up the blanket so he could take pictures of the children. This seemed to throw the firefighter "off balance" and ruin all of our efforts to reduce exposure to the event. The firefighter was deeply impacted by this.

Conclusion

Thoughtfulness and some simple, common sense guidelines can be very helpful in reducing scene distress for the families of victims. Emergency operations personnel may also be the beneficiaries of a carefully managed scene which insists on respect and dignity for the bodies of the deceased.

Chapter 5: When Children are the Survivors

There are always two choices, two paths to take.
One is easy. And its only reward is that it's easy.

Unknown

Dealing with children at an emergency scene can be extremely difficult. Having their "greater-than-life" and protective guardian die or be seriously injured will cause thoughts of extreme vulnerability and fear for their own safety. The fear of abandonment and the distress and anxiety produced by separation from parents or other important people in their lives cause many children to become terrified, inconsolable or vulnerable to shock.

Children will have different perceptions of death and dying depending on their age and developmental stage. Here is a brief synopsis of children and grief:

* **Around 3 months.** Once a child bonds with a parent by showing attachment such as fear of strangers or separation anxiety, they will show grief (Craig, 1996).

* **Up to 3 years.** Children three years old and younger, although limited in their cognitive understanding, feel and react to the death of a parent with strong emotions and confusion.

* **3-5 years.** Three to five year old children have a poor concept of time and permanence. They may view death as a temporary thing, or they may link death to sleep (Westmoreland, 1996).

* **Around 4 years.** It is not until around the age of four that a child can fully understand the concept of death. Even though their cognitive understanding is limited, younger children still feel strong emotions in the death of a parent. Significant emotions include separation anxiety - the ever present fear they will become abandoned, the uncertainty of becoming attached to someone, and guilt and hostility.

According to the American Academy of Child and Adolescent Psychiatry (1996), children may go through several stages of grief. They may regress or act younger than they really are. And because young children believe they are the cause of what happens around them, they may believe the death was caused by their wishes. For example, perhaps a child thinks or says, "I hate my baby brother, I wish he would go away." If that baby brother died of SIDS, the child who uttered the wish might feel that he caused his baby brother to "go away". Children believe that they have "magical thinking" , that is if they wish for something, it happens. This belief can create great guilt for children.

Children pick up on the feelings expressed around them. If adults are frightened, children become frightened. If adults are emotionally upset, children believe that they should be upset. Janice Harris Lord, in her book, *No Time for*

Good-byes (1994), explains that this is why nurturing is so very important for children. Explanations about what has happened may not have any meaning for children. They need much more. When dealing with children, what you do is more important than what you say. "Holding, cuddling and stroking are ways of assuring them that they are cared for" (p. 52).

When dealing with surviving children at an emergency scene, the following guidelines may be useful:

* **Limit the exposure to the scene.** Children should not be exposed to gory sights and disturbing sounds or odors. Shield them from anything that is disturbing.

* **Hold the child.** They need the physical contact with a caring human being to assure them that they will be taken care of.

* **Talk softly.** Keep voices down. Do not shout. Keep a calm and controlled demeanor.

* **Be gentle.** Avoid rough handling of a child. This is particularly important if the child has sustained injuries in an event that has killed a parent or sibling or other important person in the child's life.

* **Avoid rushing.** Slow down your movements unless the situation warrants rapid movements because of life saving considerations. Rushing may be interpreted by a child as panic on the part of the caretaker. If the helper is panicked in the child's view, then the child feels a sense of panic as well.

* **Keep the child warm.** Do not forget that shock can set in and threaten a child's physical well being.

* **Listen to the child.** If a child needs to tell the helper their experience of the event, listen carefully. But be cautious not to probe for too many details.

* **Show the child that he or she is being taken care of.** Assign someone to stay with the child. As mentioned earlier, hold the child and just be there until close relatives can be notified and respond to the scene.

* **Get close relatives to the scene.** When possible, contact close relatives to be with the child. Familiarity of people will help ease their pain. If the child is older and is adamant about seeing the parents, respect this, but try to convince the child to wait until the close relative is on scene and can be there with them.

* **Be honest.** If a child asks a question, be prepared to answer it honestly. Dr. Catherine Sanders relates that "when children are left to their own thoughts without real information, they can dream up the worst possible fears." Dr. Sanders goes on to explain the importance of being careful not to give more details than the child is equipped to process. Children can become readily confused, so it is best to "allow children to ask the questions they need to have answered" (1992, p.176).

* **Offer continued support.** Become aware of centers for grieving children in your area, and offer the information to close relatives or surviving parents.

* **Never leave a child alone.** Leaving a child alone near an accident scene, even for short periods of time, can produce a feeling of terror.
* **Avoid confusing terminology.** When talking to children it is important to avoid euphemisms. Children often take literally what is told to them. If dad "went away," the children will expect him to eventually return. Don't tell them God took a loved one away because he or she was "good" or "that God needed another angel." As a result, a child might fear being good or fear God. Explain truthfully and to the best of your ability. Children will find more comfort in truth than in an adult's attempt to hide something or create a fantasy.
* **Allow for transition time when transferring a child to another's care.** Children do not automatically transfer their bonding from one caretaker to another. It takes time to make such transitions. Emergency personnel who must transfer a child to the care of hospital staff, for instance, should not just drop off the child and go on about their business. They should, instead, stay nearby for a period of time to reassure the child that he or she will be well taken care of by the new people with whom he has just come into contact.

Conclusion

Assisting children through the shock and disruption of the death of a cherished loved one is one of the most challenging situations encountered by emergency personnel. The responsibility for the care of a child is enormous. Lasting impressions are likely to be left on that child's mind. Those impressions may have either a negative or positive effect for the remainder of that child's life. Following the simple guidelines above will help to assure that the impressions which are made on a child are positive ones.

Chapter 6: Understanding and Dealing with the Elderly

"Isn't it terrifying that we discard old people when their working life is finished and they are no longer useful? Isn't it disturbing that we cast them into old people's homes, where they die lonely and abandoned?"

Sogyal Rinpoche
(p. 9)

It is easy to stereotype the elderly as vision and hearing impaired, poor drivers and crotchety. In the emergency services profession we have our "frequent flyers" who typically are lonely elderly folks in need of attention and who call 9-1-1 at the most inopportune times. But most of these conceptions of the elderly come about because of a lack of understanding on our part.

Try to put yourself in the position of many elderly people. How would you feel if your spouse needed emergency medical care and the responders seemed more concerned about medical insurance than patient treatment? "Without gaining the trust and respect of the elderly, it is impossible to obtain an accurate history and to perform a worthwhile physical exam" (Schwartz, et al, 1984, p.163). The elderly have different views on life because they are in its final stages. Their friends are beginning to die, and they begin to lose their status in a youth oriented society. Here are just a few of the issues elderly people have to deal with:

* **Death & dying.** Their friends and family members are dying. They must also face the inevitability of their own death. The realization of death's potential in their own lives becomes apparent as their body systems slowly begin to fail. "Living Wills" and "Do Not Resuscitate" orders are among the unfortunate plans older people have to consider.

* **Great new technology vs. quality of life.** We have the means to prolong life, but is it a life worth living? Elderly people become very concerned that they will be kept alive on machines and medications, but will be unable to experience the joys of daily living, such as walking, holding a grandchild or visiting a place of interest.

* **Being stripped of one's clothing equals being stripped of one's dignity.** Your beloved wife of 50 years becomes seriously ill at home. You dial 9-1-1 and within minutes, four firefighter/medics, and two ambulance medics are in your bedroom and have your wife's clothes off of her. "Yes, but," we say , "it is all done in the name of medical care!" Surely, there must be a way to achieve medical care without disregarding the dignity of elderly people.

* **Bureaucracy.** Many people on a fixed income have to deal with

insurance, social security regulations, taxes and other governmental regulations. If you, in your old age, become unable to take care of yourself, you may be relegated to a care facility. My dad once was misdiagnosed with Alzheimer's disease. The State took away his drivers license, and he spent countless hours, days, months and years fighting the bureaucracy to get it back.

* **Loss of things we take for granted.** As body systems begin to fail, so does control. Simple things like taking a walk with a loved one, cooking, playing with a grandchild, listening to music or reading may become difficult or impossible to do.

* **Changes in appearance.** The body changes as we grow older. Hair loss, changes in bone structure, posture, physical appearance and graying hair make many elderly miss their old selves. Many are self conscious and embarrassed about their looks.

* **Loss of physical and mental function.** As the body deteriorates, in many cases, so does the mind. Simple tasks become frustrating as memories are more difficult to access and higher cognitive functions become more challenging.

* **Fear of becoming a victim of crime.** Some elderly have been brutalized by an uncaring and cruel society around them. People have stolen everything, from their retirement checks to their stocks and bonds. Violence has made their neighborhoods less safe and many elderly remain barricaded in their homes out of fear of becoming yet another victim of violence.

Unfortunately, for some elderly people the only smile or sense of caring they may receive is from emergency workers. They may, therefore, call upon emergency workers to come to their homes for what appears, on the surface, to be inconsequential situations. If emergency personnel treat them harshly, the last link to kindness may be fractured. Elderly people will then have no one to turn to when they really need help because they are fearful of angering or offending those who might respond to their call for help.

To better understand the elderly in times of emotional crisis, during the phases of high anxiety, denial and anger, keep in mind that the initial response may also include:

---

* **Disorientation**
* **Confusion**
* **Helplessness**
* **Fear**

In talking with a group of elderly widows, I found many of the same concerns addressed earlier. Words can hurt and last a lifetime. One woman shared that her family told her "You should be over this by now." She is still angry about this after two years. Other non-thinking phrases include:

* *"They led a good life."*
* *"Be thankful you still have your children"*

Many of the elderly's children do not live close by and/or may not offer much support to their aged parent.

* *"Be thankful you had a good life together."*
* *"Be thankful for the many years you had together."* I will bet that a person who has just lost their spouse of 60 years, would like to have had 61!

* *"Time will heal."*

Time helps you cope - it does not always heal.

* *"It must have been their time."*
* *"Death comes to us all."*
* *"They are in a far better place."*
* *"They are no longer in pain."*

Another woman shared (after the death of her third husband) that "More and more, I miss my first husband, the husband of 25 years, the father of my children." How could anybody know what this woman is going through? For the elderly, a loss may bring up multiple losses from their past. That is why it is so important to convey caring.

> "A broken heart is not a myth. There is firm documentation regarding this devastating loss. When we lose our mate, the person we have relied on for support, the one we have depended on in countless ways, is no longer there. The partnership is dissolved: half of us is gone"
> (Sanders, p. 139).

Pets

It is also important to understand that pets are part of the family. For the elderly, their pet may be the only "person" that conveys caring and understanding. Their pets have provided companionship, entertainment, a sense of security and joy over many years. Sometimes the pet is the last major remaining attachment to a child who has grown up and moved away from home. The elderly will grieve the loss of their pet friends as you would a family member. They may grieve for a very long time. Be sensitive, kind and understanding when a elderly person has lost a pet. Please do not tell people not to worry because they "can always get another pet". Such a statement demeans the loss they have encountered and leaves the bereaved person feeling angry and frustrated.

When death is imminent

During times of emotional crisis, such as the impending death of a loved one, a caring emergency services person should remain with the family members, particularly the elderly members of the family. If it is possible, someone should explain everything that is going on during resuscitation attempts. In most cases the elderly will stand in the background and watch you work on their loved one, and it is easy to forget about them. It is important that they understand that everything possible is being done, and that you are truthful when survival of the patient is not likely. It is important to encourage them to say their good-byes to the dying family member or friend. It is not easy to do this, but it is important. After all, it will, more than likely, be the last chance they ever get to say what they need to their loved one. The following paragraph may be used as a guide for advising family members to speak with a dying person.

"Mrs. _____, you called for the ambulance about 20 minutes ago. We have been working on your husband since our arrival. We have contacted the hospital and we have utilized a variety of medications and attempted every medical procedure available to us. I need to tell you and the other family members that your husband is not responding to anything we have done so far. We will continue our work here for a few more minutes. I am sorry, but soon we will have to stop our efforts. The hospital is directing us to do that if we do not soon see any response. Now would be a good time for you and some of the family members to gather around and say good-bye to your husband while we are still trying to revive him."

When death has occurred in the home

The following caring actions are important in dealing with the elderly when the death of a loved one has occurred in their home:

* **Be honest.** Provide the survivor feed-back during the resuscitation event. Don't just quit the efforts without keeping the survivors aware that things are not going well.

* **Ask if there is a blanket with which they would like the body covered.** Most times there is a special covering the spouse will find to cover the body. Also ask the survivor if they would like the head covered. Most times they will not.

* **Convey caring.** It's okay to say "I'm sorry." It's okay to put your hand on the survivor's shoulder.

* **Offer continued support.** Find out if there is anybody you can call for them. If they want to make the calls, be available in the room in case they are unable to finish their conversation. Don't leave them alone. Ministers, family members or close neighbors can be contacted to sit with the grieving.

* **Allow grief.** After a death has been declared, I will tell the grieving survivor that it is okay to spend time with their loved one. I've seen crying men lie down on the floor with their deceased wife to say good-

bye, to tuck them in, and reflect on their lives together. I can't imagine their grief and frustration if we didn't allow this.

* Ask to hear about their loved one. Either while gathering patient information with the spouse or waiting for someone to come stay with them, I'll ask what their husband/wife used to do for a living, or what their hobbies were. This projects an expression that you care about the deceased. It also provides great stories about the past that you probably wouldn't get reading a history book. The survivor is usually glad to share their loved one's past with you.

Conclusion

It is awfully hard to lose a family member or a good friend. People will certainly remember the experience for their lifetime. What they will also remember is the little kindness and courtesies you have shown them in one of the darkest moments of their lives.

Chapter 7: Special Considerations

Experience is not what happens to a man. It is what a man does with what happens to him.

Aldous Huxley

In attempting to cover all the possibilities of difficult situations to which emergency workers respond, special consideration needs to be given to those in which scene survivors or "VIPs" have disabilities or are "one of our own."

Because of a lack of knowledge and understanding, dealing with the disabled can cause an uncomfortable response from the emergency worker, and dealing with a scene of a known victim or survivor can have a profound impact on rescuers and their organizations. Both of these situations are discussed here.

When the "VIPs" are Disabled

Even though we are trained as "helpers," don't get sucked into an assumption that we know what a disabled person needs or wants. Probably one of the most common mistakes is to assume that disabled folks need more of your assistance than anyone else. "Disability is a social construct rather than a medical diagnosis (Mairs, 1997, p. 13)," and a person labeled "disabled" will have the same needs during an emotional crisis, and doesn't need a stereotypical social pity response from the emergency worker. There is an inherent human drive since infancy to "do it myself" and emergency responders should respect this drive in those with limited abilities. Be careful not to confuse physical differences with physical limitations. A few simple rules will ease the situation for both responder and the "VIPs."

PhysicallyLimited
   * If the "VIP" is in a wheelchair or using other equipment for mobility, ask "can I help" instead of just assuming they need help.
   * Address the physically limited person directly,not his or her companion.

Visually Limited
   * If dealing with a visually impaired "VIP," identify yourself and ask if they need assistance. Don't shout (the patient is blind, not deaf).
   * Tell the "VIP" everything that is being done and why, and what to expect.
   * If a Guide Dog is involved and injured, assign another emergency worker to care for the dog until veterinary care is available. Assure the "VIP" that everything possible is being done to help the dog.
   * If the Guide Dog is not injured, keep it as close as possible to the"VIP."
   * If you do take the blind "VIP" somewhere, let them take your arm, not vice-versa.

* A deaf "VIP" may seem alert but fail to respond to emergency responders. Do not misinterpret gestures or sounds as mental incompetence.

* Request assistance from family members or others. If verbal communication is limited, use written communication.

* If the "VIP" can read lips, be sure you face him or her when talking. Speak slowly and clearly without exaggerating your lips (this may distort words).

* Avoid statements like "I could never do what you do," or "you're so strong." Be caring without being condescending.

When the death is a suicide

Suicide is one of the best forms of one-way communication known. The person who commits suicide leaves everyone around them feeling the same feelings that may have driven him to commit suicide. Survivors often feel frustrated, angry, lost, hopeless, helpless, hapless, worthless, confused, sad, overwhelmed and uncertain of themselves. Suicide victims transmit these and other feelings to their loved ones. The most unfortunate aspect of this type of communication is that the person committing suicide does not wait for an answer. This leaves the family and friends struggling for many years to try to make sense out of a horrible tragedy.

Please be sensitive and caring to people who have encountered the suicide of a person in their lives. They need a great deal of understanding and support. The road of recovery is a difficult one for them. Most family members and friends of a suicide victim want to talk about it to some degree. Do not probe unnecessarily, but do not be afraid to discuss the loss if they seem willing to talk about it. Sometimes it is helpful to ask if they had any sense of warning that the suicide was being contemplated. If you ask with a sense of care and concern, you could inquire about whether or not there was a note or if there was something in the person's life which might have triggered the suicide. You could also ask if the family members would like to tell you anything about the life of the suicide victim. Inquire if there is anything you can do to assist the family members while you are still at the scene. Such questions are far better than "small talk" about the weather while you are waiting for the arrival of the medical examiner or for a release so that you can be returned to your normal service status.

Please remember that a suicide is treated as a "crime scene" so you generally have to keep the family and friends out of the area. You have to be careful to preserve the scene in as untouched a manner as possible. Wait for the police to advise you before allowing anyone into the scene. We need to make sure we do not make the job of the investigating officers any more difficult than it already is.

When it's "One of Our Own"

According to many emergency responder stress scales, one of the most profound situations is the line-of-duty death, suicide or serious injury of a co-worker or known person. This section will not give instruction on what to do or say, as these survivors should be treated in the same caring manner as any other survivor. What will be discussed is the importance of recognizing that these situations can cause an extreme personal stress reaction and/or even throw an organization into shock and dysfunction.

* Co-Workers as "VIPs"

Whether it's dealing with the spouse of a co-worker or the co-workers themselves, we are subconsciously reminded of our own   vulnerability. There is a bond among emergency service workers formed by the shared experiences of death and dying, and attempts to take chaotic, potentially life threatening situations and lessen their impacts on humanity. These experiences, we feel, can only be understood by our colleagues. A study on California Law Officers
found the "impact of an officer's death on co-workers is often dramatic, as exemplified by the fact that as many as three-fourths of officers involved in a critical incident may leave the force within five years (Eney, 1993, p. 1)." Besides the assistance needed for the surviving family members, the emergency service organization needs to be prepared to assist the responders and colleagues affected by the incident. All agencies should have in place a departmental policy outlining activation of stress management teams for responders in the event of co-worker injury or death.

*Known "VIPs"

It was a fall evening when I was summoned to the scene of a fatal car accident involving a teenager. The family had shown up at the scene and the Incident Commander was calling for Chaplain Services. Upon arrival, the I.C. identified the "VIP", stating that he was an older brother who had come upon the accident. After a short introduction, I began to explain to the brother the events that would be taking place (the teenager was D.O.A. and still in his car). During our conversation I began to get an uncomfortable feeling and discovered that the dead teenager was one of my teenage son's best friends. I continued with the task at hand, all the while knowing that when I came off "auto pilot" there would be incredible emotions to deal with. I was able to effectively deal with this incident because of strong support from family and departmental chaplains trained in Critical Incident Stress Management (see chapter 9 for more information on Critical Incident Stress Management programs).

I do not envy those that serve in smaller communities where the chances of responding to someone known are greatly increased. It is important to become aware of the extreme emotional impact these situations may have on yourself, your colleagues and your organization, and have support systems in place to aggressively deal with them when they occur.

Conclusion

It is impossible to adequately prepare for every potential crisis situation. That is why a set of crisis intervention principles that can be applied to virtually any situation is essential in emergency services work. The circumstances mentioned in this chapter briefly outline some of the more complex situations which may be encountered. Perhaps the brief descriptions and suggestions presented here will be a starting point for emergency organizations to develop detailed plans for complex interventions.

Chapter 8: Compassion Fatigue

"Man is the only animal that laughs and weeps; for he is the only animal that is struck by the difference between what things are and what they might have been."

Hazlitt

When I was researching material for this book, I found that there was considerable apprehension among emergency personnel about being compassionate at the scenes of tragedies. It appeared that the greatest fear expressed by emergency workers was the fear of loading another person's grief onto themselves. Most people feel that they have enough to bare in life without carrying another person's pain around with them.

I can honestly say that I do not look forward to dealing with surviving relatives while a loved one is seriously injured or when they have just died. And I do occasionally fear that emotional skeletons may be brought out of my own closet with each new tragic scene I encounter. Mental health professionals have several names for the taking on of another's grief. Vicarious traumatization, counter transference phenomena and compassion fatigue can all be described as the end result of the empathetic helping of others following a traumatic event. Hopefully this guide will help diminish some of the fear associated with scene compassion and will provide useful tools to assist in avoiding vicarious trauma.

I cannot deny that being caring at an emergency scene can add additional stress to an already stressful event. A key to responder survival, however, may be to "know when to say 'when'," and as suggested earlier, "it doesn't always have to be you" who takes on the role of survivor advocate at the emergency scene. Through an understanding and recognition of this "vicarious traumatization" or "compassion fatigue" responders can remain healthy and happy while still showing scene compassion.

Understanding Vicarious Trauma

Charles Figley, Ph.D., in his book *Compassion Fatigue* , describes the "cost of caring," and the stress that results from helping the traumatized. Dr. Figley identifies those who are vulnerable. This will assist emergency responders to help identify scenes that may produce unwanted stress. Key areas of vulnerability include:

* Empathy

"Empathy is a key factor in the induction of traumatic material from the primary to the secondary victim. Thus the process of empathizing with a traumatized person helps us to understand the person's experience of being traumatized, but, in the process, we may be traumatized as well" (p. 15).

* Past Personal Trauma

Very few of us are without past traumatic events. Everybody has personal "skeletons in their closet," and if we haven't been taking care of ourselves in our work as responders, past traumatic events can become present events. Recognize when an event is stirring up old emotions, and call for assistance to deal with the surviving family members. Remember, (I can't emphasize this enough), it doesn't always have to be you who deals with the survivors.

* Unresolved Trauma

Be sure to resolve issues bothering you. You will not be successful in emergency work, let alone compassionate, if you are carrying the baggage of unresolved issues. Whether personal or work related, it is important that, if needed, professional counseling be used. It would be difficult to identify another person's grief, if we haven't dealt with our own.

* Extraordinary Events

Dr. Figley suggests that emergency workers have the most difficulty when dealing with the pain or death of children. Extraordinary events and other overwhelming circumstances, whether or not they involve children, are, in themselves, significant factors to be aware of as producers of vicarious traumatization.

Signs and Symptoms of Vicarious Traumatization or Compassion Fatigue

If not recognized and taken care of, this "compassion fatigue" can lead to cumulative and permanent effects. Sheila Walty, Clinical Coordinator of Oregon's Critical Incident Stress Management Team, summarizes some of the common signs and symptoms of compassion fatigue that are found in printed literature (1997). They include:

> * **A feeling of not having time for yourself**
> * **Nightmares**
> * **Feeling of despair and hopelessness**
> * **Social withdrawal**
> * **Disconnection from loved ones**
> * **Increased sensitivity to violence**
> * **Cynicism about your ability to help others**
> * **Numbing**

I did this chapter on Compassion Fatigue solely because of the raised concerns about our emotional health. Vicarious traumatization has become an issue in the mental health field partly because of the counselor's duty of confidentiality. Those who work with the grieving as a profession are unable to share much of their counseling experience with others outside of the mental health professions. Fortunately, emergency workers are able to talk to each other and to their friends and family about their own pain after dealing with situations involving death and dying. Firefighters and medics who work with a partner or as a member of an engine or truck company, can share their difficulty or concern about an event. This is an advantage over most police officers who may be working alone. Responders who do work alone must make the effort to communicate and share with their comrades. When dealing with grieving people "If you have a good team approach where other members of your staff watch over you and with whom you can share your own feelings, there is very little danger in becoming involved" (Kuebler-Ross, 1997, p. 14).

Conclusion

This chapter raises an alarm that warns us all that we are vulnerable to the condition called "vicarious traumatization" or "compassion fatigue." Knowing what the condition is and how one might lessen its impact is important for the survival of those who help others.

Chapter 9:*Taking Care of Ourselves*

"I am only one, But still I am one. I cannot do everything. But still I can do something:And because I cannot do everything, I will not refuse to do the something that I can do."

Edward Everett Hale

To embark upon or continue in this job we love, and to be able to go the extra mile to show caring and compassionate service to those we serve, we must take care of ourselves. There has been much written on job stress and its reactions in the emergency services and other professions. A great deal has also been written on the topic of mitigating stress. Successful stress mitigation strategies have been developed for all of the following categories:

---

* **Education and Training**   * **Proper Nutrition**
* **Physical Exercise**   * **Faith**
* **Taking Time to Do Things You Enjoy** * **Laughter**
* **Developing Close Friendships**   * **Talking**
* **Critical Incident Stress Management** * **Respect for Others**

Education and Training

Take training seriously. "We play the way we practice." There is nothing worse than having an already stressful scene deteriorate because you or your co-workers don't know where the needed equipment is, can't get it working, or have forgotten how to do a specific task.

Educate yourselves on emergency services stress. Few emergency personnel have been trained adequately to deal with the emotionally demanding events they must manage in their day-to-day work. They are asked to perform a great many skills for which they have received excellent technical training. They can usually accomplish these with little or no difficulty. However, when it comes to recognizing and appropriately intervening in situations in which other human beings are emotionally distressed, emergency workers are at a loss. They have never been taught crisis intervention skills. They are unsure of what to do to alleviate the emotional pain of another person (Mitchell and Bray, 1990, p.85).

Know the sources of stress, their signs and symptoms, and what you can do about it if you are stressed. *Critical Incident Stress Management* (Everly and Mitchell, 1999) is an excellent resource and should be mandatory reading for all who enter emergency services careers. The book contains many excellent suggestions for maintaining healthy performance. Here are some others.

* Eat a proper diet

Eat right! Stick to a well balanced diet. Proteins are important. Cut down on the level of carbohydrates you consume. Use supplementary vitamins, especially vitamins B, C and E. Limit the intake of caffeine (always a crowd pleaser in the fire house), salt, sugar, white bread, processed foods and foods with a high fat content. Because alcohol is a depressant, avoid using it to help get through difficult times. Alcohol interferes with rapid eye movement during sleep and thus impairs the cataloging of information in the brain during sleep. The chances of getting "stuck" with unprocessed aspects of a traumatic experience are higher when alcohol is used after a traumatic event.

* Exercise

Physical exertion has been shown to be one of the best ways to mitigate stress. Numerous studies have shown that people stay healthier and perform better when they are physically fit. Physical exercise has many psychological benefits as well. People who exercise feel better about themselves. They tend to be more confident. Vigorous exercise also produces endorphins. California's Loma Linda University School of Medicine found "when you strengthen muscles and improve your level of fitness, you also condition the pituitary glands that produce endorphins and other calming chemicals," causing conditioned people to deal better with stress (Wild, 1999).

In a study on police officers, Belles & Norvell, (1993) demonstrated that subjects experienced significant reductions in psychological symptoms and improvement in mood following an exercise program. Other studies have shown exercise not only increases "positive affect" and mood state, but also that individuals who do not exercise seem to be at a greater risk of physical illness (Yeung & Hemsley, 1996, 1997). In my own research on a mandatory circuit weight training program for firefighters, the greatest changes came in the areas of perception of stress and in the symptoms the firefighters encountered after they experienced a traumatic event. The study suggested a more positive attitude accompanied physical exercise. Personnel, therefore, felt that they had the ability to contribute more to the job (Dietz, 1998).

The exercise should be organized, consistent and purposeful. Weight lifting, jogging, bicycle riding, walking, competitive sports and swimming are all excellent activities to help keep stress under control. Try to utilize exercise activities that are not directly related to the job so that there is a sense that the job does not overwhelm every aspect of our lives.

* Take Time to do Things You Enjoy

One advantage of emergency service work is that we see how fragile life can be and how quickly things can change. Make the time to enjoy life to its fullest. Plan and schedule time off to do something you really want to do, and then stick to it. Vacation, fish, boat, ski, develop a new hobby, do the things that emergency service employees are known for (because we have all that time off!). Go back to work refreshed and with vitality. Plan to do something enjoyable again on your next day off.

* Develop Close Friendships

We are social beings. There is no greater feeling than sitting with people you enjoy being with. They can provide "sounding boards" for stress, sources for humor and/or partners for activities. Develop close relationships with your spouse, kids, brothers and sisters and parents. As stated above, in the emergency services business it becomes obvious how fragile life is and how quickly loved ones can be taken from you. Sometimes it takes a quick slap in the face before you realize just how good you have it. It wasn't until I talked with the local chapter of "Parents of Murdered Children" that I realized my life could be worse and I needed to take advantage of my close family relationships.

* Laugh

"Laughter becomes a safety valve against explosion; it ensures better health because it releases some of the tension locked within our bodies" (Sanders, p. 202). Laughter has been shown to increase the secretion of catecholamines and endorphins. These chemicals reduce   pain and induce the feeling of happiness (Seigler, cited in Briand, 1999). Hang around people who are funny, attend comedy films and/or plays or read humorous books and magazines. Billy Graham once said "A keen sense of humor helps us to overlook the unbecoming, understand the unconventional, tolerate the unpleasant, overcome the unexpected, and outlast the unbearable."

Be careful with black humor. As a way of dealing with stress, some can find humor in even the most tragic of situations. This is a normal response. Try not to let such humor offend you or others, and be careful that this "firehouse humor" stays in the fire house and out of the public's eye.

* Talk

If something is bothering you, talk about it. An advantage of emergency work is that you usually have co-workers who understand your situation. Defuse or debrief after significant events in your life. This catalogues those skeletons in your closet and allows you to cope with them after significant emotional events. It is hard to take care of others if you are not taking care of yourself. As an emergency responder, find out how to activate your local Critical Incident Stress Management (CISM) team and use it. Studies show that talking after an emotional event helps speed up the recovery time. Make sure that your CISM team follows a standard model appropriate for emergency response personnel. Dr. Jeff Mitchell has developed a comprehensive, systematic and multi-tactic approach to dealing with work related stress within organizations. It is especially useful after traumatic events.

* Critical Incident Stress Management (CISM)

The "Mitchell Model" of Critical Incident Stress Management (CISM) is also called the "ICISF" model because the International Critical Incident Stress Foundation promotes it internationally. The International Critical Incident Stress Foundation is a non-profit organization that provides crisis intervention and stress management training and education as well as a range of crisis support services. It is the most widely used crisis intervention model in the world and it is the only crisis intervention model with the research to back it up. It has proven itself to be very effective with emergency workers. It is also widely used in military services, business, industry, school systems and communities. It has been applied in many disasters.

CISM is a comprehensive, systematic, and multi-tactic approach to managing traumatic stress. It has services that are provided before a tragedy occurs. It has services that are employed during a traumatic event as well as services that are utilized after a traumatic event has occurred. CISM has support services for individuals, small and large groups, families, organizations and communities.

The core components of a well-organized CISM program are:

Pre-incident preparation, education and training
On-site support programs
Individual consultations
Demobilizations for operations personnel
Crisis Management Briefings for non-operations personnel
Defusings
Critical Incident Stress Debriefings (CISD)
Family support services
Follow up services
Referral mechanisms

In the **pre-incident preparation** aspects of a CISM program, the focus is on policy development, planning, training and CISM education. **On scene support services** are those services which are provided under field conditions. Primarily they entail one-on-one support, advice to command staff and assistance to the victims of the incident. **Individual consultations** mean one-on-one support given to colleagues who are distressed by an incident. **Demobilizations** are brief informative meetings with large groups of operations personnel after their first exposure to a major incident. They help to restore personnel to normal functions or to enhance the return to home. **Crisis Management Briefings** are brief informative meetings for large groups of non-operations personnel in the aftermath of a major event within a community.

Defusings are shortened **Critical Incident Stress Debriefings** (CISD) which occur on the same day as the traumatic event. They are small group discussions of the experience. CISD is a more structured group discussion of a traumatic event . It usually takes place several days after the event and helps to put the incident in perspective so that people can return to normal functions. **Family support services** include a range of activities from family education to direct support services which are provided for the families of personnel who have experienced a traumatic event or some other stressor. **Follow up services**

can be telephone calls, visits to the work site, small group meetings and many other interventions which take place after an incident. They are designed to make sure that people are recovering from their traumatic experiences. In some cases, **referrals** for additional care may be necessary to assure full recovery.

In the brief space available here, it is impossible to do anything other than provide the briefest of overviews of CISM. It is strongly recommended that people receive appropriate training from the ICISF to properly conduct a CISM program for their organizations. Today, ICISF has about twenty different two-day training programs in the field of crisis intervention and stress management.

To contact ICISF, write or call:

ICISF
10176 Baltimore National Pike
Unit 201
Ellicott City, Maryland 21042
Phone: (410) 750-9600
Fax: (410) 750-9601
web: www.icisf.org
24- hour emergency (410) 313-2473

If your organization utilizes private mental health workers in its Employee Assistance Program, make sure they are trained in CISM. They also need to understand the unique personality of and special situations that emergency responders handle.

* Have Faith

Throughout my career in the fire service, it is has been rare to hear theology integrated into the work environment. Occasionally, God's name comes up in a stress debriefing. Some rescuers may question the meaning of a tragic situation, and wonder what God's plan is. As you continually respond to other people's tragedies, you tend to develop beliefs and/or put meaning to these events. It is up to you to develop your own faith. No one can do that for you. Some say that every event has a divine purpose. Not that God wants people to experience grief, but that every event causes something positive to happen sometime or somewhere. A relationship with God seems to add peace and understanding during difficult times. "Often it is such an exceptionally difficult situation which gives man the opportunity to grow spiritually beyond himself" (Frankl, 1959, p. 114).

* Treat Everybody With Respect

I have been lucky enough to travel and present to people the emergency "Scene Compassion" program. I always end these lectures by making every person in attendance take out their business card. On this card, I have them write CARE vertically. These letters stand for: Compassionate Assessment, Respect Everybody.

I have them do this on a business card because this is why we are in the business. When people are experiencing a significant emotional event in their lives, they want people there who care about them. Assess the scene with compassion. Are there people in the background grieving? Respect everybody. Whether the body is living or deceased, respect it as you would your closest relative. This not only leaves the permanent impression of caring to the survivors, but will assist you in facilitating any emotions encumbered by knowing you did the right thing.

Business Card

C ompassionate
A ssessment
R espect
E verybody

Chapter 10: *Things We Will Not Know*

"I am and know and will; I am knowing and willing; I know myself to be and to will; I will to be and to know."
Saint Augustine

There are so many things happening in the minds of the grieving. Things we cannot possibly know, but need to understand because they are ever present. The things going on inside people can have a positive or negative impact on our services to them. Each tragic event has its own personal history that causes feelings and behaviors only understood by those experiencing them. It was not until I began to talk with people after reconciling their tragedies that I began to understand the "things we will not know."

I watched in horror one day as a grieving husband tried to get to his dead wife after a fatal motor vehicle accident. Police officials on the scene, dealing with an already stressful situation, did not want to deal with an additional problem, the problem of a grieving husband. He was intercepted. Attempts failed to restrain him, and eventually he was thrown to the ground. After threat of handcuffs and arrest, the husband finally gave up, and stood back with the other on-lookers all the while saying "That is my wife." Much later I found out that this grieving husband had had an earlier argument with his wife. I can't imagine the guilt he must have felt for her dying without having come to some resolution. He most probably wanted to tell his wife he was sorry.

This case represents a prime example of what I am talking about. All tragedies seem to carry with them a secret known only to those most closely involved with the dead or dying. The secret is present in the lives of those we serve. We do not need to know what it is, we only need to be aware that it exists. Another way to say this is that all human behavior makes sense in the context in which it occurs. It may not make sense to us, but it makes sense to the person who is involved in the situation.

As I visit with people who have experienced sudden emotional crisis, occasionally these "little secrets" surface. As presented in the chapter on "Understanding and Dealing with the Elderly," the woman, who had cared for and watched her third husband die, began to grieve for her first husband. She shared with me that he (her first husband) was the love of her life, the father of her three children, her soul mate. They had been married for twenty-five years when he died. I believe she felt a little guilty about this. This first loss, of course, emergency responders could not have known about, but it came up when they were dealing with the latest loss.

A sixteen year-old girl had just received her driver's license and wanted to drive to her "first" party. Not only did she want to go to a party, she wanted to wear make-up. Her parents told her absolutely not. The child cleaned the house, mowed the lawn, did the dishes for a week, and softened her parents up until they gave in. The evening of the party, the parents received news that there had been a fatal accident involving their car. When they arrived at the scene, they were separated from the crowd and taken to their car for body identification. The firefighters had not done a very good job in covering the young woman, leaving her hands and arms exposed. I cannot imagine how the red fingernail polish (worn for the first time), illuminated under the scene spot lights, must have exploded out into the parent's faces, showing them that they should not have let their daughter grow up so soon. There is no way the emergency workers could have known the impact of their actions on this family. Please make every attempt to cover the entire body, so that the "little secrets" are uncovered as the survivors are ready to handle them.

My own son Justin had a reaction to his DPT inoculation that left him with mild Cerebral Palsy and a seizure disorder. He took extra nurturing and patience while we taught him sign language and worked to get him to talk, crawl, and then walk. How could anyone be expected to know this when he died? How could anyone know how much work his mother had put into his survival, only to have it suddenly taken away? This is another "secret" known to those who love him, but not to the emergency personnel.

In conclusion, it all came vividly clear while sitting at the funeral of a friend of my mother. A simple poem brought home the importance of treating everybody with respect, decency, and the dignity they deserve. It brought forth the history people have and the impact the deceased can have on survivors. Everyone is loved, whether a child or elderly widow. If they don't have a loved one with them when they die, then they may have us, the emergency responder. A grandchild stood in front of the chapel and read these words:

I Will Not Cry Tomorrow

Today we will not visit face to face
But you will hear what I m saying

When the weather gets colder
We will not watch your ferns fill up with snow
But I will plant ferns near my kitchen window
And sometimes they will wear blankets of white

In spring we will not walk in your garden to see Irises in bloom
But my garden will always know their beauty

You will not hide Easter eggs for me to find this year
But one day I will hide them for my children
And I too will let the little ones go first

In June we will not pick the strawberries you've planted
But I will grow them too and I will learn to make jam

In November we will not sit at the same table
But I will give thanks for the times that we did

This Christmas I could not ring the bell in your kitchen
But bells rang as Heaven welcomed an angel

You will not rock my children to sleep
But I promise they will know you

Today I may cry as I say good-bye
But tomorrow I will not for I have known you

Gretchen L. Keyser

APPENDICES

APPENDIX A

Sample Operational guideline
Feel free to modify this to fit your organization

Woodburn Fire District recognizes the need to care for the person(s) directly related to an emergency incident as well as mitigating the incident itself. It will be the Scene Officer in Charge's responsibility to assign an "Occupant Services" sector when they feel it is appropriate. The Fire District's Chaplains have been trained to function as the Occupant Services Sector so scene personnel can be free to handle the situation. If a Chaplain is not available then the Scene Officer will assign someone on the scene.

1.	Occupant Services Sector shall be established when dealing with civilians on the following:

A. Prolonged and/or unusual rescue operations.
B. Death/Severe injury of emergency worker.
C. Incidents involving large numbers of people.
D. Confirmed working fires in occupied buildings.
E. Multiple alarm incidents.
F. By request of Incident Commander or Officer in Charge.

2.	Occupant Services shall function as a Sector Officer under the Incident Command system.

3.	Necessary services shall be provided to those in need and Incident Command shall be continually updated.

A. Explain the actions taking place and why specific steps were taken.

B. Determine and relay destination of relatives being transported to hospitals / morgue.

C. Determine if occupant(s) [VIP] need a place to stay, then assist in making appropriate arrangements. Notify the Red Cross, Salvation Army, and / or other agencies that might be of assistance.

D. Provide for immediate transportation needs of the occupant [VIP].

E. Identify potential psychological support and / or mental health needs for the occupants [VIP] because of the emotional trauma they have experienced as a result of the incident.

F. Determine the ten most important items to the occupant, so that the District can focus it is salvage operations to those items.

G. Seek information from the occupant, such as the location of hazards, valuables, etc., that tactically might be of significance.

H. Provide immediate access to a telephone or cell phone. (Do not let VIP's do death notifications over the phone).

I. If appropriate, coordinate a walk through of the scene when cleared to do so.

J. Coordinate scene security with the occupant so that vandalism or looting does not occur after the Fire District departs.

K. Work with the proper utility companies for restoring or proper disconnect of services.

L. Identify other needs of the occupant [VIP].

APPENDIX B

Emergency Scene "Prompt" Sheet

This "prompt" sheet can be modified to fit your current system. This particular worksheet is designed for any situation from fire to EMS.

Are VIP's Identified and Separated?

Date: Incident Commander: Phone #

DISPATCH INFORMATION	SCENE ASSISTANCE		NEED HELP?	
		OK NEEDED		OK NEEDED
ADDRESS _____	Operations Explained	☐ ☐	FIRE	☐ ☐ Phone #'s
_____ ·	Phone	☐ ☐	POLICE	☐ ☐ "
	Transportation	☐ ☐	EMS	☐ ☐ "
OTHER _____	Shelter	☐ ☐	RED CROSS	☐ ☐ "
	Food	☐ ☐	UTILITIES	☐ ☐ "
	Chaplain/CISM	☐ ☐	POWER	☐ ☐ "
VICTIMS INFORMATION	Scene Walk-Through	☐ ☐	WATER	☐ ☐ "
Name Age	Scene Security	☐ ☐	NAT. GAS	☐ ☐ "

VICTIMS INFORMATION	LOCATION OF HAZARDS, VALUABLES OF TACTICAL SIGNIFICANCE
_____	ITEM AREA
_____	ITEM AREA
_____	**TEN MOST IMPORTANT ITEMS**
"VIP INFORMATION	_____ _____
_____	_____ _____
_____	_____ _____
_____	_____ _____
_____	WHERE CAN THE FAMILY BE CONTACTED?
Hospital Destination	Address Phone
_____	

APPENDIX C

**Compassion Satisfaction/Fatigue Self-Test for Helpers
(Myers, D., Wee, D. (1999). <u>Prevention of Compassion Fatigue in CISM.</u>
Presented at Fifth World Congress of Stress, Trauma and Coping in the
Emergency Services Professions, Baltimore, MD.)**

Helping others puts you in direct contact with other people's lives. As you
probably have experienced, your compassion for those you help has both
positive and negative aspects. This self-test helps you estimate your compassion
status: How much at risk you are of burnout and compassion fatigue and also
the degree of satisfaction with helping others. Consider each of the following
characteristics about you and your current situation. You can make a copy of
this test so that you can fill out the numbers and keep them for your use. Using
a pen or pencil, write in the number that honestly reflects how frequently you
experienced these characteristics in the last week, then follow the scoring
directions at the end of the self-test.

0 = Never   1 = Rarely   2=A Few Times   3 = Somewhat Often   4 = Often   5 =
Very Often

Items About You

1. I am happy.
2. I find my life satisfying.
3. I have beliefs that sustain me.
4. I feel estranged from others.
5. I find that I learn new things from those I care for.
6. I force myself to avoid certain thoughts or feeling that remind me of a
   frightening experience.
7. I find myself avoiding certain activities or situations because they
   remind me of a frightening experience.
8. I have gaps in my memory about frightening events.
9. I feel connected to others.
10. I feel calm.
11. I believe that I have a good balance between my work and my free time.
12. I have difficulty falling or staying asleep.
13. I have outbursts of anger or irritability with little provocation.
14. I am the person I always wanted to be.
15. I startle easily.
16. While working with a victim, I thought about violence against the
    perpetrator.
17. I am a sensitive person.
18. I have flashbacks connected to those I help.
19. I have good peer support when I need to work through a highly stressful
    experience.

20. I have had first-hand experience with traumatic events in my adult life.
21. I have had first-hand experience with traumatic events in my childhood.
22. I think that I need to "work through" a traumatic experience in my life.
23. I think that I need more close friends.
24. I think that there is no one to talk with about highly stressful experiences.
25. I have concluded that I work too hard for my own good.
26. Working with those I help brings me a great deal of satisfaction.
27. I feel invigorated after working with those I help.
28. I am frightened of things a person I helped has said or done to me.
29. I experience troubling dreams similar to those I help.
30. I have happy thoughts about those I help and how I could help them.
31. I have experienced intrusive thoughts of times with especially difficult people I helped.
32. I have suddenly and involuntarily recalled a frightening experience while working with a person I helped.
33. I am pre-occupied with more than one person I help.
34. I am losing sleep over a person I help's traumatic experiences.
35. I have joyful feelings about how I can help the victims I work with.
36. I think that I might have been "infected" by the traumatic stress of those I help.
37. I think that I might be positively "innoculated" by the traumatic stress of those I help.
38. I remind myself to be less concerned about the well being of those I help.
39. I have felt trapped by my work as a helper.
40. I have a sense of helplessness associated with working with those I help.
41. I have felt "on edge" about various things and I attribute this to working with certain people I help.
42. I wish that I could avoid working with some people I help.
43. Some people I help are particularly enjoyable to work with.
44. I have been in danger working with people I help.
45. I feel that some people I help dislike me personally.

Items About Being a Helper and Your Helping Environment

46. I like my work as a helper.
47. I feel like I have the tools and resources that I need to do my work as a helper.
48. I have felt weak, tired, run down as a result of my work as helper.
49. I have felt depressed as a result of my work as a helper.
50. I have thoughts that I am a "success" as a helper.
51. I am unsuccessful at separating helping from personal life.
52. I enjoy my co-workers.
53. I depend on my co-workers to help me when I need it.
54. My co-workers can depend on me for help when they need it.
55. I trust my co-workers.
56. I feel little compassion toward most of my co-workers.

57. I am pleased with how I am able to keep up with helping technology.
58. I feel I am working more for the money/prestige than for personal fulfillment.
59. Although I have to do paperwork that I don't like, I still have time to work with those I help.
60. I find it difficult separating my personal life from my helper life.
61. I am pleased with how I am able to keep up with helping techniques and protocols.
62. I have a sense of worthlessness/disillusionment/resentment associated with my role as a helper.
63. I have thoughts that I am a "failure" as a helper.
64. I have thoughts that I am not succeeding at achieving my life goals.
65. I have to deal with bureaucratic, unimportant tasks in my work as a helper.
66. I plan to be a helper for a long time.

Scoring Instructions:

Please note that research is ongoing on this scale and the following scores should be used as a guide, not confirmatory information. Cut points are theoretically derived and should be used with caution and only for educational purposes.

1. Be certain you respond to all items.

2. Mark the items for scoring:

a. Circle the following 23 items: 4,6-8, 12, 13, 15, 16, 18, 20-22, 28, 29, 31-34, 36, 38-40, 44.

b. Put a check by the following 16 items: 17, 23-25, 41, 42, 45, 48, 49, 51, 56, 58, 60, 62-65.

c. Put an X by the following 26 items: 1-3, 5, 9-11, 14, 19, 26, 27, 30, 35, 37, 43, 46, 47, 50, 52-55, 57, 59, 61, 66.

3. Add the numbers you wrote next to the items for each set of items and note:

    a. Your potential for Compassion Satisfaction (X): 118 and above = extremely high potential; 100-117 = high potential; 82-99 = good potential; 64-81= modest potential; below 63 = low potential.

    b. Your risk for Burnout (check): 36 or less = extremely low risk; 37-50 = moderate risk; 51-75 = high risk; 76 - 85 = extremely high risk.

c. Your risk for Compassion Fatigue (circle): 26 or less = extremely low risk; 27-30 = low risk; 31-35 = moderate risk; 36-40 = high risk; 41 or more = extremely high risk.

Adapted with permission from Figley, C.R., (1995). Compassion Fatigue, New York: Brunner/Mazel © B. Hudnall Stamm, Traumatic Stress Research Group, 1995-1999 http://www.isu.edu/~bhstamm/rural-care.htm.

The following self-test has been modified from it's original previous format to provide personal educational results quickly. This is only a guide and not confirmatory information.

Consider the questions honestly and score each response as follows:

0=Never 1 = Rarely 2=A Few Times 3 = Somewhat Often 4 = Often 5 = Very Often

Potential for Compassion Satisfaction
SCORE

* I am happy.

* I find my life satisfying.

* I have beliefs that sustain me.

* I find that I learn new things form those I care for.

* I feel connected to others.

* I feel calm.

* I believe that I have good balance between my work and my free time.

* I am the person I always wanted to be.

* I have good peer support when I need to work through a highly stressful experience.

* Working with those I help brings me a great deal of satisfaction.

* I feel invigorated after working with those I help.

* I have happy thoughts about those I help and how I could help them.

* I have joyful feelings about how I can help the victims I work with.

* I think that I might be positively "inoculated" by the traumatic stress of those I help.

* Some people I help are particularly enjoyable to work with.

* I like my work as a helper.

* I feel that I have the tools and resources that I need to do my work as a

helper.

* I have thoughts that I am a "success" as a helper.
    * I enjoy my co-workers.

* I depend on my co-workers to help me when I need it.

* My co-workers can depend on me for help when they need it.

* I trust my co-workers.

* I am pleased with how I am able to keep up with helping technology.

* Although I have to do paperwork that I don't like, I still have time to work with those I help.

* I am pleased with how I am able to keep up with helping techniques and protocols.

* I plan to be a helper for a long time.

Calculate your potential for compassion satisfaction by adding the scores:
118 and above	extremely high potential
100-117	high potential
82-99	good potential
64-81	modest potential
below 63	low potential

0 = Never   1= Rarely   2=A Few Times   3 = Somewhat Often   4 = Often   5 = Very Often

Risk for Burnout   **SCORE**

* I am a sensitive person.

* I think that I need more close friends.

* I think that there is no one to talk with about highly stressful experiences.

* I have concluded that I work too hard for my won good.

* I have felt "on edge" abut various things and I attribute this to working with certain people I help.

*   I wish that I could avoid working with some people I help.

*   I feel that some people I help dislike me personally.
*   I have felt weak, tired, run down as a result of my work as a helper.

*   I have felt depressed as a result of my work as a helper.

*   I am unsuccessful at separating helping form personal life.

*   I feel little compassion toward most of my co-workers.

*   I feel I am working more for the money/prestige than for personal fulfillment.

*   I find it difficult separating my personal life from my helper life.

*   I have a sense of worthlessness/disillusionment/resentment associated with my role as a helper.

*   I have thoughts that I am a "failure" as a helper.

*   I have thoughts that I am not succeeding at achieving my life goals.

*   I have to deal with bureaucratic, unimportant tasks in my work as a helper.

Your risk for burnout by adding your scores:

36 0r less	extremely low risk
37-50	moderate risk
51-75	high risk
76-85	extremely high risk

0 = Never   1 = Rarely   2=A Few Times   3 = Somewhat Often   4 = Often   5 = Very Often

Risk for Compassion Fatigue   SCORE

*   I feel estranged from others.

*   I force myself to avoid certain thoughts or feelings that remind me of a frightening experience.

*   I find myself avoiding certain activities or situations because they remind me of a frightening experience.

*   I have gaps in my memory about frightening events.

*   I have difficulty falling or staying asleep.

*   I have outbursts of anger or irritability with little provocation.

*   I startle easily.

*   While working with a victim, I thought about violence against the perpetrator.

*   I have flashbacks connected to those I help.

*   I have had first-hand experience with traumatic events in my adult life.

*   I have had first-hand experience with traumatic events in my childhood.

*   I think that I need to "work through" a traumatic experience in my life.

*   I am frightened of things a person I helped has said or done to me.

*   I experience troubling dreams similar to those I help.

*   I have experienced intrusive thoughts of times with especially difficult people I helped.

*   I have suddenly and involuntarily recalled a frightening experience while working with a person.

*   I am pre-occupied with more than one person I helped.

*   I am losing sleep over a person I help's traumatic experiences.

*   I think that I might have been "infected" by the traumatic stress of those I help.

*   I remind myself to be less concerned about the well being of those I help.

*   I have felt trapped by my work as a helper.

*   I have a sense of hopelessness associated with working with those I help.

*   I have been in danger working with people I help.

Your risk for Compassion Fatigue by adding your scores:

26 0r less	extremely low risk
27-30	low risk
31-35	moderate risk
36-40	high risk
41 or more	extremely high risk

This questionnaire is adapted from a presentation by Diane Myers, RN, MSN and David F. Wee, MSSW, at the *Fifth World congress of Stress, Trauma and Coping in the Emergency Services Professions,* in Baltimore, Maryland. It has been modified from it's original version to provide emergency responders a quick and simple evaluating tool to measure the likelihood of burnout and compassion fatigue in their jobs. Ms. Myers and Mr. Wee adapted their original questionnaire with permission from Figley, C.R., (1995). *Compassion Fatigue,* New York: Brunner/Mazel.

REFERENCES

American Academy of Child and Adolescent Psychology. (1996, May). *Children on grief* [on-line]. http://www.psych.med.umich.edu/web/ascap/ (visited 1997, Sept. 1, 1977).

Barrett, M. (1995, July). death notification. Parents of Murdered Children Newsletter. (Vol 14, No. 7). Portland.

Belles, D., Norvel, N. (1993). Psychological and physical benefits of circuit weight training in law enforcement personnel. Journal of Consulting and Clinical Psychology, 61. 520-525.

Briand, S.J., (1999). Take two chuckles and call me in the morning [on-line]. http://web2.airmail.net/cybervyl/research.htm (visited 1999, March 10).

Carlson, R. (1997). Don't sweat the small stuff...and it's all small stuff. New York: Hyperion.

Chapman Dick, L. (1996). Impact on law enforcement and EMS personnel. In Doka, K.J. (Ed.) Living with grief after sudden loss. (pp. 53-71). Bristol, PA: Taylor & Francis.

Craig, G. (1996). Human development. (7th ed.). New Jersey: Prentice Hall.

Dietz, T.W. (1998). The evaluation of psychological benefits of circuit training on Woodburn firefighters. Unpublished applied statistics essay, Warner Pacific College, Portland.

Eney, V. (1993). Line of duty death (concepts and issues paper). IACP national law enforcement policy center. Alexandria, Virginia

Everly, G.S and Mitchell (1999). Critical Incident Stress Management - CISM: a new era and standard of care in crisis intervention, 2nd edition. Ellicott City, MD: Chevron

Figley, C.R. (1995). Compassion fatigue, coping with secondary traumatic stress disorder in those who treat the traumatized. Bristol, PA: Brunner/Mazel.

Frankl, V.E. (1959). Man's search for meaning: An introduction to logotherapy. New York: Beacon.

Fry, W.F. (1977). The respiratory components of mirthful laughter. Journal of Biological Psychology, 19, 39-50.

Kuebler-Ross, E. (1997). <u>On death and dying.</u> New York: Touchstone.

Kuebler-Ross, E. ((1997). <u>Questions & answers on death and dying.</u> NewYork:Touchstone.

Lord, J.H. (1994). <u>No time for goodbyes.</u> (4th ed.). Ventura, CA: Pathfinder Publishing.

Mairs, N. (1996). <u>Waist-high in the world.</u> Boston: Beacon Press.

Mitchell J.T., & Bray, G. (1990). <u>Emergency services stress.</u> Englewood Cliffs, New Jersey: Prentice Hall.

Mitchell, J. T., & Resnik, H.L.P. (1986). <u>Emergency response to crisis.</u> Englewood cliffs, NJ: Prentice Hall

Redmond, L.M. (1996). Sudden violent death. In Doka, K.J. (Ed.) <u>Living with grief after sudden loss.</u> (pp. 53-71). Bristol, PA: Taylor & Francis.

Rinpoche, S. (1994). <u>The Tibetan book of living and dying.</u> San Francisco, CA: Harper.

Sanders, C.M. (1992). <u>Surviving grief...and learning to live again.</u> New York: John Wiley & sons, Inc.

Schwartz, G., Bosker, G., Grigsby, J. (1984). <u>Geriatric emergencies.</u> Bowie, Maryland: Robert J. Brady Co.

Walty, S. (1997, Fall). Vicarious traumatization. <u>The Critical Response; a newsletter of the Oregon Critical Response Team.</u> Portland, OR.

Westmoreland, P. (1996, Spring). Coping with death; Helping students grieve. <u>Childhood Education.</u> 157-160.

Wild, R., (1999, April). Lift weights, lose stress. <u>Muscle Media.</u> 84-85.

Yeung, R., Hemsley, D. (1996). Effects of personality and acute exercise on mood states. <u>Personality and Individual Differences, 20.</u> 545-550.

Yeung, R., Hemsley, D. (1997). Personality, exercise and psychological well- being: static relationships in the community. <u>Personality and Individual differences, 22.</u> 47-53.